PHYSICIAN,
HEAL
THY *Financial* SELF

PHYSICIAN, HEAL THY *Financial* SELF

Achieving Mastery Over the
Finances of Your Practice

JILL ARENA

Dear Mary,
Thanks for the trust you've placed in us over the years— it's always a pleasure to work with you!

This is likely all review for you, but perhaps there's a pearl or two?

Cheers,
Jill

E&M Coding Sheet by Code USA (code-usa.net)

This book is dedicated to all physicians, and anyone else who gives their lives over to the process of healing their brothers and sisters. You have my utmost respect and heartfelt gratitude for the difference you make in this world.

CONTENTS

FIGURES

All figures are available for download from Health e Practices, with our compliments, at HealthePS.com

Acknowledgements & Gratitude

It takes a village.

To Amy Gillcrist, MD, Saramati Krisha, MD, and Chad Morse, MD, who are clients, friends, and in part, the people this book was written for. Thanks to each of you for your encouragement, feedback, and suggestions to make this book better for your colleagues. (Chad, the Oxford commas in this paragraph are for you.) I appreciate all of you. It's fun to walk with you as you run your practices. Here's to many more successful years!

To my friend and PEX partner Chris Kiklas, my thanks for the opening line of the book. You really got my passion about the book, and my stand for physicians to be financially healthy. In reflecting that back one Saturday morning, you gave me the perfect opener and I'm so glad that the world of transformation has your leadership.

To the entire team at Health e Practices, my thanks all day and every day. A girl couldn't ask for a better team – you ladies and gents really rock. I love how each of you are dedicated to our physician clients and their success. A lot of what I've learned in working with all of you appears here. Thanks for being part of the magic.

To my Medical and Dental Advisory Team family – you know who you are – thanks for always pulling me to bigger things. Thanks for your leadership in our medical community, and thanks for being my mastermind group. I cherish our meetings and our friendships, and look forward to the next seven years. Cheers!

To national consultant and leadership guru Stephen Franey, my thanks for your commentary, your thought partnership, and your friendship. Wisdom I've gleaned from you appears throughout this book. Given what you've seen in your career, it's an honor and a privilege to work with you.

To my entrepreneurial muse and dear friend, Warren Johnson, thanks for saying those things about how I should grow my company that make my stomach hurt. And thanks for always encouraging me to do them anyway. You've added to my personal and professional journey in so many ways… next round of Rusty Nails are on me.

To my leadership partner in crime, Craig Wright, MD, my thanks to you for your constant example of effective, classy, and humble leadership. You walk the talk. I am grateful every day for your thought partnership. It is so much fun to watch you work, and to see your commitment to physician leaders of the future. So delighted to work with you on that initiative. Let's grow some.

To my dear friend Samantha Beatty, with whom there is another book waiting to be written. (That one we keep chuckling about…) Your friendship means the world. So delighted to celebrate you and to watch your healthcare career blossom over the years, Madame Chief Operating Officer.

To my dear friend and retired pharmacist and informaticist Nan Robertson; my brother's mother-in-law, businesswoman Donna Shaw; my published-author mother Judy Schmatjen; and the best college intern I've ever had, Isabelle Whitlock: thanks to each of you for your eagle eyes, your edits, and your content suggestions for making this book as good as it can be.

To my brother, Marc Schmatjen, the many times published author who walked with me through the entire process of bringing this book to the world. Thank you. This would simply not have happened without you. And I thought the writing was the hard part!

With love to Mom & Dad, who taught me that hard work is the path to a well-lived life, and who have been my greatest supporters, even when they didn't really understand what I do for a living. Now I think maybe they do.

And finally, to my creative powerhouse of a daughter Bella, who inspires me every day to be the best version of myself. I love you great big bunches times infinity.

Introduction

I am all about money. Your money. From your practice, to be exact.

I've spent nearly thirty years working with physicians and medical groups all over the country, and I continue to find independent, savvy, smart physicians who take great care of others – their patients – and not such great care of their financial selves.

This is a book about financial self-care at the practice level. It is for independent physicians, and employed physicians who want their practices to perform better financially. It is for physicians who have a mortgage (or two), student loans, personal debt, maybe some kids to put through college, and retirement accounts to fund. If you've taken care of all of that, this book isn't for you. If you're still working on it, pull up a chair and your laptop, and let's get you financially healthy.

How this book works:

I want this to be easy. I know you received little (or in most cases, no) business training while you were going to medical school. When I ask if there were any business or finance classes before medical school graduation, everyone I've asked said, "Nope!" And yet, many come out of residency to run their own practices – which amount to businesses – most of which produce millions of dollars each year. And... you're supposed to magically know how to deal with all of that? Maybe you've been working with a group and you've just been offered partnership. How will you know if it's a good deal? Or, you've been employed with a practice for a while, and now you find yourself in a leadership role – Medical Director or board member – and you now have a fiduciary duty to your group. But, what exactly does that mean?

I realize you have precious little time left over in your day after being in clinic or the OR, and you need this to be as efficient AND comprehensive as possible. You need to know how to oversee your practice's finances in a couple hours a month. Challenge accepted! We can do it together.

This book is designed to break it down for you – you can read it all the way through, and then take on whichever assignments seem relevant, or you can work your way through each chapter and do the Real World Work at the end of each chapter in the order presented.

Either way, you'll learn something new about how to run your business, and what questions you need to be asking of your team.

The medical community has been very good to me for thirty years. This book is intended as my gift back to that community. My pay-it-forward. It may be too basic for some, in which case, you can share it with your partners or your heir apparent as you develop them. You can use it as a primer to get your partners on the same page, and as a toolkit or playbook for your group's development.

At the core, I want to see medical practices thrive, and I want to see physicians as empowered leaders within their organizations, whether they are large medical groups, or solo practices. I want this tool to give you mastery over the finances of your practice.

The high-level questions are organized into five major sections:

Section I) Data: Get with "What is So" – Where are you starting?

Section II) Money: Assets, Budgets, and Cash Flow – Where are you going?

Section III) Planning: Financial, Strategic, and Retirement – How will you get there?

Section IV) People: Staff, Extenders, and Partners – Who is going with you?

Section V) Wrapping it All Up – Did you get where you needed to be?

For ease of use, since many of these terms may be new to you, I've **bolded** the important ones, and they are listed in the Glossary of Terms in the back of the book. This should serve as a quick reference as you're coming up to speed.

All the figures in this book are available for your immediate use from the Health e Practices team, with our compliments. Download them at HealthePS.com.

Again, you can read all the way through, or skip to a pertinent section for a quick education. So, let's jump in!

Section I

DATA

Get with "What is So"

Where are you starting?

Chapter 1

<u>Overview of Your Practice Finances</u>

Sometimes the scariest thing about finances is not knowing where you are. Is your practice doing okay? Are you well compensated in relation to your peers? Are your practice expenses in line with the rest of the industry? All of these questions are easy to answer when you have good data.

The first thing to know (or find out) is which accounting system your practice uses. Many groups use **QuickBooks**, which has become the gold standard for small to medium-sized businesses of any kind. If you do use **QuickBooks**, is it local (also called "desktop version") or is it the online version? We still run into bookkeepers and accountants who prefer the local version, which is the older one. I strongly recommend the online version! That way, **QuickBooks** takes care of security and backups for you, at no extra cost. It's their business – they'll do it right. Count on a monthly expense of $50 – $75, which is far less than keeping an accounting program on a server and needing to pay for backups and security yourself. Either way, figure out which system you use, and get yourself logged in. [Please note that I have no financial relationship with **QuickBooks**, other than being a long-time customer of theirs – I simply find their products to be best in class.]

The first step in getting connected to your practice finances are the financial reports. How do you get reports? Are they generated by a bookkeeper or your manager? Regardless of the answer, you should be able to log in and run your own reports as well. That way, if you have a question in the future, you're not dependent on someone else to get the data you need.

[Author's note: Throughout this book, I have referred to the businessperson who helps run your practice as "manager," "office manager," "clinic manager," and "practice administrator" interchangeably. Titles are important to some people, and generally "manager" is an entry-level leader, while "administrator" or "practice administrator" is a higher-level MBA type who would run a group of $5 million or more in annual revenues.]

As you become more proficient in reading and using financial reports, you can depend on others to generate them for you on a regular basis. If you work as part of a larger group or health system, there should be someone in the accounting department designated to run reports for you. There may be some office politics to work through here if you are requesting more direct access.

The two most common and useful reports are the **Balance Sheet** and the **Profit and Loss (or Income) Statement**. The **Balance Sheet** is a listing of your assets (what you have – think cash in your business checking account, equipment in your clinic), and your liabilities (what you owe – think credit card balances, loans). The **Balance Sheet** is a listing of those, and it is a snapshot in time. It shows the balance in all accounts as of any given day. We usually run these every few months, and they should be reviewed every 6 months as you're getting a handle on things, and every year thereafter. You can use this series of snapshots to track your financial progress over time. Make sure things are moving in the right direction (like loan balances going down if you're making regular payments) and that the accounts all look current, and you know what they are. Ask questions about any that are unfamiliar.

Here is an example of a clinic's **Balance Sheet**. Your clinic's should look very similar, and in fact, if you have a financial planner, he or she may have prepared one of these for you personally. In that case, the difference between your assets and your liabilities is your net worth. In a business sense, that's called "Owner's Equity" or just "Equity."

BALANCE SHEET

June 20XX

ASSETS

Cash & Equivalents

Columbia Bank	$	148,898
First Citizens	$	370,502
Spark Credit Card	$	(20,318)
Bill.com Money Out Clearing	$	1,688
Petty Cash	$	903
Cash in transit - per Billing	$	58,684
Total Cash & Equivalents	**$**	**560,357**

Accounts Receivable

Billing Receivable	$	66,022
Other Receivable	$	3,207
Total Accounts Receivable	**$**	**69,229**

Other Current Assets

Prepaid Expenses	$	6,435
Total Current Assets	**$**	**636,021**

Fixed Assets

Gross Fixed Asset Purchases	$	2,031,842
Accumulated Amortization and Depreciation	$	(1,227,868)
Total Fixed Assets	**$**	**803,974**
Total Non-Current Assets	**$**	**803,974**
Total Assets	**$**	**1,439,995**

LIABILITIES

Accounts Payable

Accounts Payable	$	321,551

Other Current Liabilities

Payroll Related Liabilities	$	2,965
Sales & Excise Taxes Payable	$	7,402
Accrued Expenses	$	928
Gift Certificates and Customer Prepayment	$	37,190

Revenue - unallocated (NexTech)	$ 9,808
Total Other Current Liabilities	**$ 58,293**
Total Current Liabilities	**$ 379,844**
Long Term Debt	
Third Party Debt	$ 726,964
Shareholder Loans	$ 294,941
Total Long Term Debt	**$ 1,021,905**
Total Liabilities	**$ 1,401,748**
EQUITY	
Retained Earnings	
Retained Earnings	$ 64,868
Current Earnings	
Current Year Earnings	$ 11,684
Other Equity	
Equity - Dr. Jane Smith	$ (116,409)
Dividends Paid	$ (34,003)
Opening Balance Adjustments	$ 112,107
Total Other Equity	**$ (38,305)**
Total Equity	**$ 38,247**
Total Liabilities & Equity	**$ 1,439,995**

Figure 1 – **Balance Sheet**

Your **Profit and Loss Statement (P&L)** or **Income Statement** is a great document for understanding what's happened over a period of time, and for tracking performance. I recommend running this once a month, and reviewing it against your budget, which we'll get to later. The **Income Statement** is a detail of all of the income that came in during the time period, and all of the expenses you incurred in the same time period. The amount left over is called "**net income**" and in most private practices is the amount that gets split up between the owners. In your personal finances, this is what's left over in your checking account at the end of the month, ostensibly available for investment or paying down debt, or that trip to Italy you've been contemplating.

The practice expenses are also frequently called "overhead" and can be calculated as a percentage of **net revenue**. This allows you to understand what percentage of your **net revenue** (cash collected less **refunds** issued to patients and insurance companies) is paid out to operate your clinic before you pay yourself. Most groups range between 35-65% overhead with primary care being at the higher end of the spectrum. If your overhead is higher than 55-60%, don't despair. There is likely a lot of room for improvement! We'll get to the expense reduction ideas in the next section.

There are many finance and accounting terms that get thrown around and are largely misunderstood. Let's clear some of that up:

Gross Revenue or **Gross Income** or **Top Line Revenue** – this is how much cash landed in your bank account. Plain and simple.

Gross Charges are something else entirely – that's what got billed to the insurance companies and patients. Depending upon your **conversion factor**, which is the amount your billing system bills out for each **Relative Value Unit (RVU)**, this may or may not be a realistic number. DO NOT expect to collect this much money – you won't. We'll get into that more as we delve into the billing and collections process a bit later.

Net Revenue – this is **Gross Revenue** less **refunds** issued to insurance companies and patients.

Total Expenses – this is all of the money that left the bank account to pay for staff, rent, medical supplies, and any other expense to run the clinic. This DOES NOT include compensation for the physicians.

Net Income or **Bottom Line** or **Bottom-Line Income** – this is **Net Revenue** less all expenses paid to run the clinic, before the doctors are paid.

Overhead Percentage – this is VERY FREQUENTLY miscalculated or misquoted. The CORRECT way to calculate it is:

Overhead Percentage = **Total Expenses**
                                          Net Revenue

This is also the source of huge bragging rights if your percentage is low (<50%). If that's true for you, brag on!

ACME Family Medicine & Integrative Health
Profit and Loss
January - April, 20XX

		Jan 20XX		Feb 20XX		Mar 20XX		Apr 20XX		Total
Income										
Monthly Charges		140,749.00		143,849.00		125,912.00		87,927.00		498,437.00
Insurance Adjustments		-53,246.49		-46,672.06		-57,180.19		-46,651.44		-203,750.18
Revenue Deposit		0.00		0.00		0.00		0.00		0.00
Total Monthly Charges	$	87,502.51	$	97,176.94	$	68,731.81	$	41,275.56	$	294,686.82
Patient Refunds		-193.50		-474.55		193.50		-382.07		-856.62
Physicians Incentive Program								3,931.44		3,931.44
Sales						160.91				160.91
Taxes & Licenses										0.00
City of ACME Revenue Expense		-175.00		-194.35		-137.46		-82.55		-589.36
ACME State Department of Revenue Expense		-1,575.05		-2,040.71		-1,237.18		-742.96		-5,595.90
Total Taxes & Licenses	-$	1,750.05	-$	2,235.06	-$	1,374.64	-$	825.51	-$	6,185.26
Vitamin Revenue		-118.32				25.75				-92.57
Total Income	$	85,440.64	$	94,467.33	$	67,737.33	$	43,999.42	$	291,644.72
Gross Profit	$	85,440.64	$	94,467.33	$	67,737.33	$	43,999.42	$	291,644.72
Expenses										
Consulting Fees		7,114.89		6,326.38		5,375.02		7,150.79		25,967.08
Contractors		3,554.16		612.24		204.68		532.25		4,903.33
Interest Bank Equipment Loan		247.41		242.39						489.80
Interest Bank Line of Credit		199.42		1,296.00						1,495.42
Medical Supplies		3,316.97		234.91		122.16		1,989.69		5,663.73
Office Equipment Under $2,500										0.00
Office Equipment Lease		224.66		308.10		228.92		230.60		992.28
Total Office Equipment Under $2,500	$	224.66	$	308.10	$	228.92	$	230.60	$	992.28
Office/General Administrative Expenses										0.00
Accounting Fees								850.00		850.00
Bank Charges & Fees		191.75		64.45		59.00		58.00		373.20
Continuing Education		617.00		5,607.00		763.22		617.00		7,604.22
Credit Card Fees		584.14		945.33		673.93		977.41		3,180.81
Dues and Memberships								71.00		71.00
Janitorial		675.00		793.52		600.00		600.00		2,668.52
Meals & Entertainment		952.90		1,462.11		718.37		251.72		3,385.10
Office Supplies		1,174.10		194.46		755.80		252.32		2,376.68
Office Supplies & Software		993.58		997.99		1,411.98		188.03		3,591.58
Other Business Expenses		533.75		710.57		782.88		297.48		2,324.68
Physicians Insurance		4.61		914.76		914.76		914.76		2,748.89
Reimbursements		0.00								0.00
Travel						49.17				49.17
Utilities		934.50		1,086.95		1,487.00		546.73		4,055.18
Total Office/General Administrative Expenses	$	6,661.33	$	12,777.14	$	8,216.11	$	5,624.45	$	33,279.03
Payroll Expenses		17.50		17.50		15.00		17.50		67.50
Company Contributions										0.00
Retirement		761.21		1,692.93		1,600.30		1,647.29		5,701.73
Total Company Contributions	$	761.21	$	1,692.93	$	1,600.30	$	1,647.29	$	5,701.73
Employee Benefits		169.24								169.24
Taxes		2,351.92		2,206.92		2,075.40		2,339.00		8,973.24
Wages		21,039.29		22,655.01		21,526.74		24,145.04		89,366.08
Total Payroll Expenses	$	24,339.16	$	26,572.36	$	25,217.44	$	28,148.83	$	104,277.79
Rent & Lease		5,999.87		5,756.42		5,756.42		6,012.95		23,525.66

8

Rent Income		-1,500.00							-1,500.00
Total Rent & Lease	$	4,499.87	$	5,756.42	$	5,756.42	$	6,012.95	$	22,025.66
Repairs & Maintenance						229.53				229.53
Total Expenses	$	50,157.87	$	54,125.94	$	45,350.28	$	49,689.56	$	199,323.65
Net Operating Income	$	35,282.77	$	40,341.39	$	22,387.05	-$	5,690.14	$	92,321.07
Other Income										
Other Miscellaneous Income								4,390.33		4,390.33
Total Other Income	$	0.00	$	0.00	$	0.00	$	4,390.33	$	4,390.33
Total Other Expenses	$	0.00	$	0.00	$	0.00	$	0.00	$	0.00
Net Other Income	$	0.00	$	0.00	$	0.00	$	4,390.33	$	4,390.33
Net Income	$	35,282.77	$	40,341.39	$	22,387.05	-$	1,299.81	$	96,711.40

Figure 2 – **Income Statement**

So, now that we've got a handle on how to get the reports that we need, how do we interpret them? More on that in the next couple of chapters.

Real World Work – Overview of Your Practice Finances:

1) Log in to your accounting system yourself – if you can't remember your login, get it refreshed and put it in your password vault. If you don't have one, get one assigned for you so you'll have it in the future. If you work in a large group that has an accounting department, request a copy and find out who you are to contact in the future when you want reports.

SPECIAL NOTE for private practices: Verify that you or one of your physician partners is the Master Administrator on the account – this function should ALWAYS be held by an owner, NEVER an employee, EVEN if that person is your spouse. This keeps you in control of your financial data whenever there is turnover in employees, and there will be. I've had groups locked out of their own financial data, and needing to recreate months or years' worth of data because a disgruntled employee left and refused to give them access. If you don't do anything else as a product of reading this book, PLEASE do this one thing.

2) Run the **Balance Sheet** as of the end of last month – this can be found under Reports in **QuickBooks**, and you can enter the date you want to see.

3) Run the **Profit and Loss statement** as of the end of last month – also found under Reports in **QuickBooks**, and you'll need to enter a date range (usually last month or year-to-date).

4) Review them and begin to note any questions. Discuss with the person in your practice who has responsibility for the finance function. If they discourage you in any way from doing this review, find a new finance person. (See Chapter 5 on Embezzlers.)

Chapter 2

<u>A Deeper Dive on Your Profit and Loss</u>

Understand where your money comes from and where it goes

We are going to dig deeper into the **Profit and Loss Statement**, as it is a powerful and informative tool to track your performance. As stated earlier, the **Balance Sheet** should be run every few months, as it won't change much. The **Profit and Loss** is your friend and it will tell you all kinds of stories about what's happening financially, and it will help you to know where to focus to improve performance.

In order to improve **bottom line** financial performance in any business, you can do three things. You can increase revenue (increase the amount of money coming in) or decrease expenses (reduce the amount of money going out) or, better yet, do BOTH!

<u>Increase Revenue</u>

First, let's look at what comes in.

For medical practices to increase income, there are several steps to take. My top three favorite ways to increase income in a group are:

1. Improve coding
2. Add a medical scribe
3. Renegotiate contracts and update credentialing

You'll note that none of these require you to work harder. This is about working smarter and getting paid for everything you do.

Coding: First of all, improving coding is a must. I can hear your deep sigh… so many coding seminars… so many rules to remember… so much BS! Yes, it is. And, it's how you get paid, and it's made deliberately complex and onerous by the insurance companies in hopes that you'll leave money on the table. Instead of doing that, let's figure it out and win the game! Studies show that approximately 80% of visits are under-coded. 80%! That means that 80% of the time, you're giving the insurance company a big discount instead of getting paid fully for what you've done for your patients. Let's not do that anymore. Let's fix that!

To break that down, if you are under-coding office visits, let's assume that instead of a 99214 (which was the level of service you delivered), you coded a 99213 (which is presently valued at 0.97 **RVU's** LESS than a 99214), either because you didn't document everything, or because in the back of your mind, you were worried about a coding audit. In most markets, that difference is worth about $52. Let's imagine you give the insurance companies $52 every time you see a patient. Let's imagine you see 80 patients a week. That's $4,160 a week or $216,320 per year that you're giving the insurance companies! I'd like YOU to get that money instead, because you provided a 99214 level of service to your patients.

How can you improve your coding? This isn't a book about coding (there are many that have already been written), but I will strongly suggest that you have a coding review. Make sure the coding specialist you're using is not the "hellfire-and-brimstone-code-conservatively-so-you-never-get-audited" type – that will just put you back where you started. Look for a coder who is appropriately detailed and somewhat aggressive on checking your documentation,

12

and coaching you on what level is supported by your current documentation, and what could help get it up to the next level of coding with another bullet point or two. My favorite one-page coding guide is here (visit code-usa.net to download this guide in all its colorful glory):

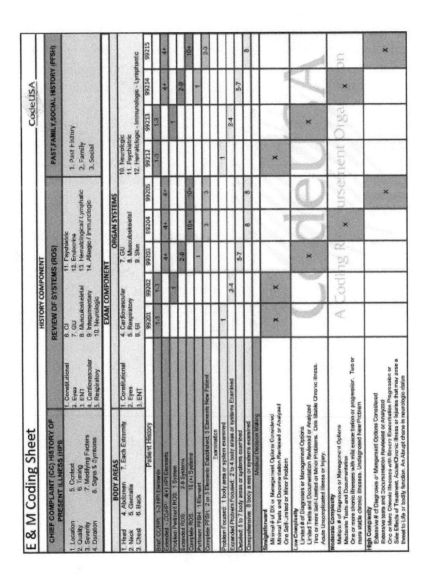

Figure 3 – E&M Coding Sheet

Or, you may decide that it pays to have a **Certified Professional Coder (CPC)** as an employee who can review all of your chart notes and code them for you. This allows you to step out of the game, minimize the risk, and give yourself a $216,320 raise! Even if you deduct the cost of approximately $60,000 for the salary and benefits for the **CPC**, you're still money ahead. And, you've left a huge headache behind. Again, vet your **CPC** carefully – you want one whose attitude is to go to bat for you, NOT to avoid an audit at all costs. If you're coding and documenting correctly, the documentation will support the code. Your hard work will be "right coded" and you can rest assured that you will prevail in the unlikely event of an audit.

[Author's note: I was not able to find any published statistics on the percentage of clinics that experience a full-blown Medicare audit, but my educated guess is that it's very low. In thirty years, I've known of only one clinic personally that went through one, and it was in relation to a larger DOJ investigation.]

Your **CPC** or your **revenue cycle manager** should be able to produce coding distribution graphs for you. I recommend reviewing a distribution of new and established patient visits (99201-99205 and 99212-99215) for a month's time. Compare that to another month out in the future, once you've changed your coding or employed a **CPC**. You can then calculate the **Return on Investment** (more on that in Chapter 3) if you've hired someone, so you can rest assured that it was a good investment, and that you're money ahead.

Coding Distribution
May 20XX

	99202	99203	99204	99205	TOTAL	99211	99212	99213	99214	99215	TOTAL
Dr. A	21	53	0	0	74	0	11	40	1	0	52
Dr. B	13	78	2	0	93	0	10	60	2	0	72
Dr. C	2	30	6	0	38	0	3	59	41	0	103
Dr. D	9	21	17	0	47	0	36	49	28	0	113
Dr. E	12	51	2	0	65	2	43	55	7	0	107

Percentages

	99202	99203	99204	99205		99211	99212	99213	99214	99215	
Dr. A	28%	72%	0%	0%	100%	0%	21%	77%	2%	0%	100%
Dr. B	14%	84%	2%	0%	100%	0%	14%	83%	3%	0%	100%
Dr. C	5%	79%	16%	0%	100%	0%	3%	57%	40%	0%	100%
Dr. D	19%	45%	36%	0%	100%	0%	32%	43%	25%	0%	100%
Dr. E	18%	78%	3%	0%	100%	2%	40%	51%	7%	0%	100%

Figure 4a – Coding Distribution Chart

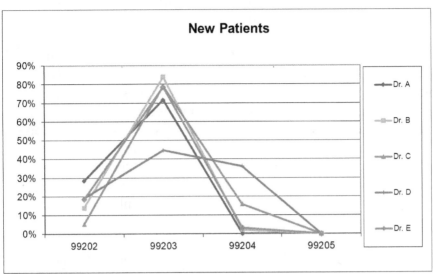

Figure 4b – Coding Distribution Graph – New Patients

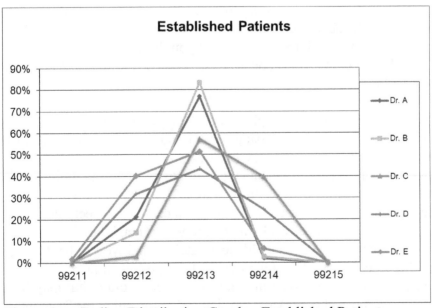

Figure 4c – Coding Distribution Graph – Established Patients

Scribes: Documentation brings us to my next recommendation – hire a medical scribe. Everyone who sees patients should have a scribe. I am convinced that when trained and used appropriately, medical scribes more than pay for themselves, and they relieve you of most of the time-consuming (and painful) logistics of documentation.

Our clients who have implemented scribes have seen large increases in revenue (in one family practice group it was 37% year over year), and corresponding large decreases in physician time spent documenting. Best of all, patients are left feeling like they got more time with the physicians (in reality, they didn't, they just perceive it as more time, because the physician isn't dividing time in the exam room between the patient and the computer), and the physicians get to finish their work day earlier. I've described it as a win-win-win, and it's my favorite operational intervention on the ambulatory side of the world today.

Some caveats about scribes – you DO need to train them, and spend time with them to bring them up to speed and to allow them to learn how you work. You should expect to spend 2-3 months giving them regular feedback. They cannot read your mind at first. After three months, if it's still not working for you, check yourself. Did you give your scribe feedback regularly? Were you specific? Did you do it in real time? If not, go back and do so. If you did all of these things, and it's still not getting you good results, perhaps it's time to look for a new scribe.

Many scribes in the marketplace today are young, bright students on their way to medical or nursing school and who need some clinical experience. This is a great way for them to get it, and for you to get a wicked-smart scribe to document your visits. You are training the next generation of medical professionals, which should leave you feeling good about your contribution. You can also expect that they'll be with you on average about 21 months. Then, they'll be off to medical school – you should celebrate! – and you'll be training another one. If you'd prefer to avoid this type of turnover, you can hire a "career scribe" who may not turn over as often, but may be a bit slower. Your choice. Most physicians I know enjoy the 21 months, and then begin training again so they always have a high caliber scribe. They understand the investment they're making.

16

A high caliber scribe should allow you to touch the computer only to sign the note after review. They should also reduce your documentation time by 2-3 hours per day, and they should allow you to see 3-5 more patients in the same number of office hours. We see this time and again with practices that implement scribes. Those who make the investment of time and energy more than pay for the scribe, and they unburden themselves of yet another onerous task.

These last two suggestions have been to add staff! I can hear you asking: Isn't that expensive? Yes. And, if done well, the additional income generated by having these folks working for you should more than pay for the additional expense. You will have delegated two unpleasant tasks, and you'll be earning more money. You have heard the old saw, "Have everyone working at the top of their licensure." If you are spending your time researching which codes to use from a long list, or if you are typing in large parts of your chart notes, this is NOT functioning anywhere close to the top of your licensure. Go ahead and let those tasks go.

Contracts: My third suggestion for increasing income is to review and renegotiate your contracts with the insurance companies in your market. The first step in doing that is recognizing who your major payers are (usually 12-15 in any major market) and seeing where your current contracts are. In doing this over the years for many clients, we've developed a contracting matrix to capture all of the critical contract details, and to keep them organized in one place. This makes it easy to know when you need to revisit them in the future. We recommend reviewing them once a year and requesting a raise. Your costs are going up all of the time, and the worst they can say is "no."

CONTRACT MATRIX

Specialty / Health Plan — Type of Benefit Plan	CMS Year (E&M codes)	Conversion Factor	Year	Type	Adjusted	Withhold	Non-Conforming	CF	92012	99203	15823	(columns condensed for size)	15823	67924	Average
Commercial															
Plan #1	2017 Fixed Year Medicare Physician Fee Schedule GPCI Adjusted	215.00%	2017	MPFS	Yes	0%	Yes	$35.89	$191.56	$239.22	$1,360.65	###	$1,357.95	$1,434.12	$764.51
Plan #2	2017 Cigna RBRVS GPCI Adjusted	204.00%		Proprietary	Yes	0%		Prop				###			Prop
Plan #3a								Other				###			$-
Plan #3b								Other				###			$-
Plan #4a	2017 RVU Non GPCI adjusted	$77.00	2017	RVU	No	0%		$77.00	$185.57	$234.85	$1,325.17	###	$1,325.17	$1,370.60	$744.17
Plan #4b	2017 RVU Non GPCI adjusted	$75.00	2017	RVU	No	0%		$75.00	$180.75	$228.75	$1,290.75	###	$1,290.75	$1,335.00	$724.84
Plan #5a	2016 CMS RVU Non GPCI	$76.00	2016	RVU	No	0%		$76.00	$182.40	$231.04	$1,306.44	###	$1,306.44	$1,352.04	$733.89
Plan #5b	2016 CMS RVU/16A Non GPCI	$78.00	2016	RVU	No	0%		$78.00	$187.20	$237.12	$1,340.82	###	$1,340.82	$1,387.62	$753.21
Plan #5c	TriCare Fee Schedule	100%	2020	Proprietary	No		Yes	Prop				###			Prop
Plan #5d												###			
Plan #6								Other				###			$-
Plan #7	2016 RBRVS No GPCI	$75.00	2018	RVU	No	0%		$75.00	$186.00	$228.75	$1,302.75	###	$1,302.75	$1,350.00	$730.31
Plan #8a	2017 CMS RBRVS	$76.25	2017	RVU	Yes	0%		$76.25	$189.30	$236.39	$1,344.59	###	$1,341.92	$1,397.43	$755.49
Plan #8b												###			
Plan #8c								Other				###			$-
Plan #9a	2017 CMS RBRVS	$77.50	2017	RVU	Yes	0%		$77.50	$192.40	$240.27	$1,366.63	###	$1,363.92	$1,420.34	$767.87
Plan #9b	2017 CMS RBRVS	$76.00	2017	RVU	Yes	0%		$76.00	$188.68	$235.62	$1,340.18	###	$1,337.52	$1,392.85	$753.01
Plan #10								Other				###			$-
Plan #11								Other				###			$-
Plan #11a												###			
Plan #11b												###			
Plan #12a	2018 CMS RBRVS	213.25%	2018	RVU	Yes	0%		$36.00	$196.73	$238.87	$1,370.65	###	$1,369.08	$1,426.88	$769.05
Plan #12b	2016 CMS RBRVS	211.71%	2016	RVU	Yes	0%		$35.80	$186.73	$233.11	$1,329.66	###	$1,327.49	$1,383.15	$747.31
Plan #13								Other				###			$-
Medicare															
Straight Medicare															
Plan #14	Current Medicare	100%	2019	MPFS	No	0%	Yes	$36.04	$89.74	$109.92	$626.00	###	$626.36	$654.47	$352.12
Plan #15	Humana's 005-5973 fee schedule	100%	2016	Proprietary	No	0%		Prop				###			Prop
Plan #16	2016 Medicare Fee Schedule Non-GPCI / Local CMS	110%	2016	MPFS	Yes	0%		$35.80	$94.52	$119.73	$677.02	###	$677.02	$700.65	$380.32
Plan #17	Current Medicare Physician Fee Schedule	110%	2019	MPFS	No	0%		$36.04	$102.01	$123.46	$707.89	###	$707.89	$743.61	$398.53
Plan #18	Current Medicare Physician Fee Schedule 5% Withhold	110%	2019	MPFS	Yes	5%		$36.04	$98.71	$120.91	$688.60	###	$689.00	$715.92	$387.33
Plan #19	Current Medicare GPCI	110%	2019	MPFS	No	0%		$36.04	$93.78	$114.87	$654.17	###	$654.55	$683.92	$367.97
Plan #20	Current Medicare GPCI	110%	2019	MPFS	Yes	0%		$36.04	$102.01	$123.46	$707.29	###	$707.29	$743.61	$398.53
Plan #21	Current Medicare Physician Fee Schedule	105%	2019	MPFS	Yes	0%		$36.04	$97.37	$117.85	$675.71	###	$675.14	$709.81	$380.41
		110%	2019	MPFS	No	0%		$36.04	$98.71	$120.91	$688.60	###	$689.00	$715.92	$387.33
Medicaid															
Plan #22	2016 CMS RBRVS GPCI Adjusted 10% Withhold	$36.00	2018	RVU	Yes	10%		$36.00	$83.03	$100.81	$578.55	###	$577.80	$602.19	$324.56
Plan #23								Other				###			$-

Figure 5 – Contract Matrix

Doing this consistently every year will alert the insurance plans that you are serious about your business, you are organized, and that you will be back. In this case, the squeaky wheel gets the grease. Ask for that raise! If you're not confident doing this yourself, hire it out. There are many consultants and attorneys who specialize in insurance contract renegotiations. A few thousand dollars to one of these specialists should net you many thousands of dollars in return.

In general, we review contracts and read for the following:

- Effective Date – When does the contract start?

- Term – How long is it good for and does it automatically renew? ("**Evergreen contract**")

- Specific Product Lines – Most plans have a commercial line of business, and one for Medicare and sometimes even one for Medicaid – which one are you being offered? Perhaps multiples?

- Termination Clause – How do you (or they) end the contract? Some of these are tricky. Read carefully. This becomes important as you reach capacity and want to "strategically prune" the insurance plans that your clinic contracts with.

- **Timely Filing Deadline** – How long do you have to submit a claim from the date of service? (The shortest ones we see are 90 days; the longest are 365.) If you surpass this date, THEY WILL NOT PAY YOU. Getting your charges in within a day or two is best practice, and assures that you will not lose money due to **timely filing** rejections, so long as your billing team is on it.

- **Resource Based Relative Value System (RBRVS) Year** – This is critical to understanding how much they're proposing to pay you. The contract will list which year of the **RBRVS** is being proposed. Each year the Centers for Medicare & Medicaid Services (CMS) publishes a new **RBRVS** schedule, which lists the **Relative Value Units (RVU's)** paid for any given CPT code. These change from one year to the next, so it's important to know which year's table they're proposing. It's also important to do a weighted analysis using your personal distribution of CPT codes, as sometimes given a shift in **RBRVS years**, something that looks like a raise may actually be a pay cut.

  If nothing in that last paragraph made sense to you, then you are likely losing out on thousands of dollars each year. Hire this part out. Again, a small investment can yield huge dividends. Make certain the person you hire can do a weighted analysis and ask them to show you one they have done for a previous client. It should be a huge spreadsheet that looks something like the figure below. You should also request at the outset that they send you a final report showing the increases they've been able to negotiate for you and an estimated value of that increase over the coming year. If they hesitate to do that, find another consultant. Any consultant worth his or her salt will be anxious to tell you EXACTLY how much of an increase they won for you. (And they should be a bit gleeful about it too!)

- **Conversion Factor** – This is the amount they are going to pay you per **RVU**. Generally, this is somewhere between $40 – $70 depending on the insurance company, your market, and your specialty.

- Gag Clause – These used to be more prevalent, and we always strike them. This would include any language that precludes you from talking about the plan above and beyond a reasonable confidentiality clause.

- Medical Malpractice Insurance Requirements – Most plans will require that you carry a minimum amount of Medical Malpractice insurance. In many cases this is $1 million per occurrence / $3 million in aggregate. If you have any questions about this, ask your med mal company what the community standard is for limits in your area. You do not want to be the highest insured in your community; this only paints a big target on your back in the event a malpractice suit is filed that even remotely involves your practice. Attorneys will always seek out the deepest pockets, and if you carry $3M/$5M in a community where everyone else carries $1M/$3M, the attorneys will be focused on you. And not in a good way.

- General Insurance Requirements – Some plans will also stipulate that you carry a minimum amount of general or **"property and casualty"** insurance. Your insurance broker can help to assure that you have adequate coverage in place. It helps to share that section of the contract with them, as some plans will have a requirement of what your insurer's rating needs to be, so your broker can sort that out.

- Bill for Non-covered Services – This one is especially important for anyone planning to transition to concierge medicine, as this is the backbone of that revenue model. Be sure there is explicit language allowing you to offer non-covered services to your patients and, provided they know in advance that it's not a covered service, you can bill them directly. Be sure the health plan will not forbid that kind of direct commerce.

RBRVS Analysis										
Specialty	E&M codes			(columns condensed for size)						
Health Plan Type of Benefit Plan	Conversion Factor	CF	92012	99203	15823 ## ## ## ## ## ## ##	15821	67924			Average
	Commercial									
Plan #1										
Plan #1	215.00%	$35.89	$191.56	$239.22	$1,360.65 ## ## ## ## ## ## ##	$1,357.95	$1,414.12			$764.51
Plan #2										
Plan #2	204.00%	Prop					Prop			Prop
Plan #3										
Plan #3a		Other								$-
Plan #3b		Other								$-
Plan #4										
Plan #4a	$77.00	$77.00	$185.57	$234.85	$1,325.17 ## ## ## ## ## ## ##	$1,325.17	$1,370.60			$744.17
Plan #4b	$75.00	$75.00	$180.75	$228.75	$1,290.75 ## ## ## ## ## ## ##	$1,290.75	$1,335.00			$724.84
Plan #5										
Plan #5a										
Plan #5b	$76.00	$76.00	$182.40	$231.04	$1,306.44 ## ## ## ## ## ## ##	$1,306.44	$1,352.04			$733.89
Plan #5c	$78.00	$78.00	$187.20	$237.12	$1,340.82 ## ## ## ## ## ## ##	$1,340.82	$1,387.62			$753.21
Plan #5d	100%	Prop								Prop
Plan #6										
Plan #6		Other								$-
Plan #7										
Plan #7	$75.00	$75.00	$186.00	$228.75	$1,302.75 ## ## ## ## ## ## ##	$1,302.75	$1,350.00			$730.31
Plan #8										
Plan #8a										
Plan #8b	$76.25	$76.25	$189.30	$236.39	$1,344.59 ## ## ## ## ## ## ##	$1,341.92	$1,397.43			$755.49
Plan #8c		Other								$-
Plan #9										
Plan #9a	$77.50	$77.50	$192.40	$240.27	$1,366.63 ## ## ## ## ## ## ##	$1,363.92	$1,420.34			$767.87
Plan #9b	$76.00	$76.00	$188.68	$235.62	$1,340.18 ## ## ## ## ## ## ##	$1,337.52	$1,392.85			$753.01
Plan #10		Other								$-

Plan	%	Label						
Plan #11								
Plan #11a		Other						$-
Plan #11b		Other						$-
Plan #12								
Plan #12a	213.25%		$36.00	$196.73	$238.87	$1,370.85	## ## ## ## ## ## ## ##	$1,369.08 $1,426.88	$769.05
Plan #12b	211.71%		$35.80	$186.73	$233.11	$1,329.66	## ## ## ## ## ## ## ##	$1,327.49 $1,383.15	$747.31
Plan #13								
Plan #13		Other						$-
Medicare								
Straight Medicare	100%		$36.04	$89.74	$109.92	$626.00	## ## ## ## ## ## ##	$626.36 $654.47	$352.12
Plan #14	106%	Prop						Prop
Plan #15	110%		$35.80	$94.52	$119.73	$677.02	## ## ## ## ## ## ##	$677.02 $700.65	$380.32
Plan #16	110%		$36.04	$102.01	$123.46	$707.89	## ## ## ## ## ## ##	$707.29 $743.61	$398.53
Plan #17	110%		$36.04	$98.71	$120.91	$688.60	## ## ## ## ## ## ##	$689.00 $719.92	$387.33
Plan #18	110%		$36.04	$93.78	$114.87	$654.17	## ## ## ## ## ## ##	$654.55 $683.92	$367.97
Plan #19	110%		$36.04	$102.01	$123.46	$707.89	## ## ## ## ## ## ##	$707.29 $743.61	$398.53
Plan #20	105%		$36.04	$97.37	$117.85	$675.71	## ## ## ## ## ## ##	$675.14 $709.81	$380.41
Plan #21	110%		$36.04	$98.71	$120.91	$688.60	## ## ## ## ## ## ##	$689.00 $719.92	$387.33
Medicaid								
Plan #22	$36.00		$36.00	$83.03	$100.81	$578.55	## ## ## ## ## ## ##	$577.80 $602.19	$324.56
Plan #23		Other						$-

Figure 6 – **RBRVS** Analysis

The contracting process can seem arduous and overwhelming. The first time you go through it, you'll have a steep learning curve. I encourage you to lean into it… this is the foundation of how you get paid. The number of **RVU's** you bill out times the **conversion factor** on your contracts equals the amount of money the insurance companies will pay you.

Many clinics we are called into have not reviewed their contracts for 5, 8, even 10 years. I'm certain that your expenses have been going up over that time period. Your employees probably got raises (if not, we'll visit that later too), and if you're not renegotiating your contracts, you are tacitly agreeing to take home less pay each year. Don't.

Decrease Expenses

Now, let's shift gears and talk about reducing expenses. While you are online in your accounting system looking at the **P&L** – take each line item, and click on the number which will take you into the detail. This can be alarming at first, especially if the numbers seem really big in relation to what you're used to seeing. Perhaps you've reviewed your household finances, but seeing $50,000 in payroll expenses seems out of control. It's all a matter of perspective, which is why it's so important to get grounded in what is "normal" for your business. In the next chapter, we'll go over budgets, which is how you define normal.

For now, when you're in **QuickBooks**, click into each line item (click on the amount – usually highlighted in blue and underlined) and review the payments. Check which vendors are being paid in each category. Do you know them? What products or services do you receive from them? Who checks that all of those products are received and that amounts ordered are appropriate? Does the expense total look right to you for a month's time? If not, where do you go to get detailed answers? These are great questions to review with your manager. If there are not processes in place, insist on some new ones.

As you get into the expense section in more depth, you'll notice that there are some expenses that are the same each month. Some examples are rent, some types of insurance, subscription services, etc. They are necessary to run the business and the amounts don't change. We generally refer to those as **Fixed Expenses**.

Some expenses you'll see will move up and down based on how busy the clinic is or how much volume goes through in a month. We call those **Variable Expenses**, and some examples are medical supplies, injectables, and office supplies.

Finally, some expenses have components that are both Fixed and Variable. Payroll (or staff) Expense is my favorite example of an expense that has both components. Generally, you need a front office person and a Medical Assistant in the office regardless of how many patients you see, so that component is a somewhat fixed cost. As you get busier, you might add more support staff in different areas, which creates a bit of a variable cost, so frequently, we say half of the payroll expense is fixed and half is variable.

Once you have begun to dig in and review your expenses, you'll get a sense for where the money is going. You may begin to ask yourself if your practice's expenses are reasonable and how they stack up against other groups in your area. For this type of information, we always recommend that groups use the Cost & Productivity Surveys from the Medical Group Management Association (MGMA), and information on those can be found at mgma.com.

[Please note that I have no financial relationship with MGMA other than having been a member of the organization and having earned my Fellowship from their college. I find their data sets and reports to be best in class and utilize them frequently for benchmarking our clients' financial performance.]

If your clinic participates in the data and submits your information, you will receive a copy of the report for free. If not, they are available for purchase on their website, and can be very helpful in benchmarking and creating goals for your clinic's financial performance. The participation can seem onerous at first, and it will take a few hours, but the more groups who respond and participate, the better the data set is as a whole. And, the data you'll get access to will be a set that you can use repeatedly.

In general, the data is divided by subspecialty, geographic region, group type (single or multi-specialty, hospital owned or private) and by group size. This way, you can get to data that is useful and pertinent to you. Many consultants have access to these reports, and they can help you take the first step to participating so that you get the reports for free. Now you've stepped into a new realm of benchmarking and measuring your financial performance.

Real World Work – Profit and Loss:

1) Get ahold of your coding data. Look at how you've coded 99201-99205 and 99212-99215 over the past year. If your usage graphs peak at 201 or 213, you likely have room to improve your coding. Find a coder to help!

2) Take the next step with getting a scribe. If you've not considered it, begin your research. If you've researched, reach out to a scribe company, or post an ad yourself and start the hiring process. If you have a scribe that isn't working so well, check yourself and your feedback, and fix that, or get a new scribe. If you have a fabulous scribe, take him or her out for a nice lunch and say, "thanks, you're doing a great job!"

3) Find your insurance contracts. Set up a matrix like the one shown in Figure 5, and if you have **RBRVS years** that are more than a year or two back in time, get those babies renegotiated. Every day that you wait is costing you money that you deserve to be paid. If you are hesitating at all about doing this yourself, hire it out. Now.

[I realize this is a lot. Don't quit now! This is BIG real work. It will take time. It will pay dividends. I promise. Do it for your own financial wellness.]

Section II

MONEY

Assets, Budgets, and Cash Flow

Where are you going?

Chapter 3

<u>Budgets and Financial Tools</u>

The creation of the budget is one of the most powerful things you can do to track the financial progress of your business. Just like we wouldn't dream of driving somewhere unknown without our favorite nav program, why would we drive our business without knowing where we're going? The easiest way to create a budget is to look back at what you already know. You can begin with the **Profit and Loss Statement** that you already downloaded. I normally suggest taking a look at what happened during the last calendar year, or for the prior 12 months if you're in the latter half of the year.

If that's in Excel, you can have the program do a lot of the work for you. I typically take the annual total and divide by 12 to get a monthly average. You can then set up columns for each month of the coming year, and copy the monthly average in to start. Then you can go through and make assumptions about what will change. Is your practice growing, and will your revenue increase? Or, perhaps growth has been a bit flat, so you can keep it consistent with last year. Or, if you have a partner leaving, you'll want to adjust. You get the picture.

I'd suggest looking at your **Gross Revenue** and **Refunds** by month for the prior year, and matching them into your new budget. Many practices have seasonal fluctuations, including decreased volumes in the summer (nice weather, and everyone cancels their appointments) and surgical practices see an uptick at the end of the year when everyone's trying to get their procedures done since they've met their **calendar year deductible**. Speaking of deductibles, you will likely observe a dip in cash flow between February and April as many patients have not yet met that sneaky little deductible. Since the claims go to insurance first, cash is slowed on the way in. Most practices see that rebound and then return to normal amounts in May and June. We lovingly refer to this as "Deductible Season."

Take a look at any expenses that are paid quarterly or annually (medical malpractice insurance is usually billed quarterly) and also check to see if your payroll is run monthly, semi-monthly or bi-weekly. If bi-weekly, you'll need to figure out which two (or three) months in your upcoming year will be "3 payroll months" and adjust the budget accordingly. I typically recommend companies do semi-monthly payroll just to smooth out these differences.

You can scan the prior year's **P&L** for any other oddities, and research. (This is a great exercise even if you're not writing a budget at the moment.) Find out what they are, if they will recur, and then add them into your budget in the appropriate month. Perhaps you have a subscription for some software that you pay annually, or some other anomaly.

Once you have created your budget in Excel, you can then request that it be loaded into **QuickBooks** or your accounting program so that you may generate reports that compare your **budget to actual** performance. Once your budget is loaded in **QuickBooks**, run reports by going to Reports: Business Overview: Budget Overview OR **Budget to Actuals**.

Now you've got a powerful tool at your fingertips! Great job.

How do you use this powerful tool? Variance analysis. In analyzing any variance from budget, you want to ascertain if the dollar amount variance is large enough to warrant further investigation, and also if the percentage variance is large enough. For instance, if your overall revenue is $2 million for the year and you are under budget by $20,000, that is only a 1% variance, and you would likely not be concerned. On the other hand, if your annual budget for office supplies is $40,000, and you are over by $20,000, that would be a 50% overage, and definitely something to investigate. So, the same

$20,000 amount would be treated differently from a management perspective.

You can see that it is important to set your review thresholds for amounts that are material to you. This can be stated as "$5,000 AND 5%." This means that in the $2 million example, the revenue variance would NOT be reviewed, since it is under the percent threshold. The office supply variance would be highlighted, reviewed and researched so you could understand that variance, since it exceeds both thresholds. Why did you spend $20,000 more on office supplies than you had planned? This is all in the spirit of understanding what's happening within your business. It is a good place to get curious.

I generally review a **Budget to Actual profit and loss report** for both dollar amount and percentage variance, and highlight any that are over my threshold for review. I'll add a note for comments, so that if you are sharing this with partners, or other leaders in the practice (or if your manager or administrator is preparing it for you), you've got space to make comments and explain variances. Below is what the finished product looks like, and it should be fairly self-explanatory once you're done. This should allow you to move through the report quickly and efficiently, discuss any important items, make plans to adjust accordingly, and move on, confident that you've managed any sudden shifts or unexpected items. You can use that information to inform the upcoming year's budget too.

ACME Medical Group
Budget vs. Actual: 20XX
January - December 20XX

	Actual	Total Budget	$ Variance	% Variance
Income				
4000 Capitation Revenue	30,258.25	26,292.00	3,966.25	115.09%
4030 Fees			0.00	
4070 Patient - Membership Fees	1,116,539.90	1,395,901.00	(279,361.10)	79.99%
4500 Patient - Office Visit Revenue	203,064.89	244,420.00	(41,355.11)	83.08%
4550 Patient - Program Fees	18,203.75	45,828.00	(27,624.25)	39.72%
Total 4030 Fees	$ 1,337,808.54	$ 1,686,149.00	$ (348,340.46)	79.34%
4100 Consulting Revenue	307,713.40	399,250.00	(91,536.60)	77.07%
4551 Exercise Program Income	10,245.96		10,245.96	
4600 Insurance Payment	1,375,675.59	1,113,108.00	262,567.59	123.59%
4700 Copayments	4,514.49	1,944.00	2,570.49	232.23%
4850 Technology Income	178,715.68	207,649.00	(28,933.32)	86.07%
4855 Billing Service Income	26,104.17	51,300.00	(25,195.83)	50.89%
4950 Medical Records Copies	1,286.50	3,409.00	(2,122.50)	37.74%
Total Income	$ 3,272,322.58	$ 3,489,101.00	$ (216,778.42)	93.79%
Expenses				
4250 Patient Refunds	17,067.20	11,433.00	5,634.20	149.28%
5000 Advertising	26,024.98	60,764.00	(34,739.02)	42.83%
5050 Answering Service	5,753.77	9,520.00	(3,766.23)	60.44%
5075 Copier Lease and Maintenance	933.23	0.00	933.23	
5080 Telephone Maintenance & Lease		0.00	0.00	
5085 Business Development Expenses		3,600.00	(3,600.00)	0.00%
5090 Recruitment	164.85	300.00	(135.15)	54.95%
5095 Software Subscription Fees	57,001.48	54,760.00	2,241.48	104.09%
5100 Salaries	1,488,513.31	1,539,663.00	(51,149.69)	96.68%
5200 Payroll Service	4,447.32	10,551.00	(6,103.68)	42.15%
5300 Payroll Taxes	127,033.20	117,016.00	10,017.20	108.56%
5410 Credit Card Fees	31,704.67	18,316.00	13,388.67	173.10%
5980 Retirement Plan Expenses	3,021.82	2,616.00	405.82	115.51%
5990 Non-Elective Contribution to 401(k)	0.00		0.00	
6010 Flexible Spending Account	927.10	1,284.00	(356.90)	72.20%
6015 Gifts & Floral	1,085.08	3,846.00	(2,760.92)	28.21%
6021 Special Events	350.00	21,469.00	(21,119.00)	1.63%
6025 Charitable Contributions	1,000.00	4,320.00	(3,320.00)	23.15%
6120 Bank Service Charges	2,912.65	8,273.00	(5,360.35)	35.21%
6160 Dues and Subscriptions	10,664.00	11,988.00	(1,324.00)	88.96%
6170 Equipment Rental	3,948.60	3,000.00	948.60	131.62%
6180 Insurance			0.00	
6000 Dental	13,497.96	13,860.00	(362.04)	97.39%
6020 Liability Insurance	2,030.98	3,360.00	(1,329.02)	60.45%
6030 Life/Disability	17,807.97	13,752.00	4,055.97	129.49%
6040 Malpractice Insurance	45,273.66	63,900.00	(18,626.34)	70.85%
6050 Medical	91,976.64	107,712.00	(15,735.36)	85.39%
6060 Work Comp	6,861.41	2,244.00	4,617.41	305.77%
6070 Accident	262.30		262.30	
Total 6180 Insurance	$ 177,710.92	$ 204,828.00	$ (27,117.08)	86.76%
6200 Interest Expense	21,287.24		21,287.24	
6210 Line of Credit Interest	12,180.30		12,180.30	
6220 Loan Interest - SBA Loan	5,073.05		5,073.05	
Total 6200 Interest Expense	$ 38,540.59	$ -	$ 38,540.59	
6211 Interest - SBP LOC	9,174.37		9,174.37	
6212 Interest - SBP Small Loan	933.70		933.70	

	Actual	Budget	Variance	%
6213 Interest - SBP Loan	7,077.41		7,077.41	
6230 Licenses and Permits	734.00	9,000.00	(8,266.00)	8.16%
6235 Marketing	7,163.32	13,950.00	(6,786.68)	51.35%
6240 Miscellaneous	5,000.00	0.00	5,000.00	
6250 Postage and Delivery	10,533.23	35,851.00	(25,317.77)	29.38%
6260 Printing & Reproduction	7,873.76	8,796.00	(922.24)	89.52%
6270 Professional Fees	4,297.15	1,524.00	2,773.15	281.97%
6280 Legal Fees	4,222.00	3,996.00	226.00	105.66%
6285 Accounting	34,708.71	17,160.00	17,548.71	202.27%
6286 Consulting	15,282.25	5,400.00	9,882.25	283.00%
6287 Website	750.00		750.00	
Total 6270 Professional Fees	$ 59,260.11	$ 28,080.00	$ 31,180.11	211.04%
6290 Rent	206,687.19	179,508.00	27,179.19	115.14%
6291 Garbage Service	1,505.06	1,800.00	(294.94)	83.61%
6292 Janitorial Service	5,214.05	5,832.00	(617.95)	89.40%
6293 Biohazard	2,074.56		2,074.56	
6295 Rent - Colocation Facility	7,691.74		7,691.74	
6300 Repairs			0.00	
6310 Building Repairs	476.41		476.41	
6320 Computer Repairs	594.49		594.49	
6330 Equipment Repairs		1,200.00	(1,200.00)	0.00%
Total 6300 Repairs	$ 1,070.90	$ 1,200.00	$ (129.10)	89.24%
6340 Telephone	48,656.03	58,920.00	(10,263.97)	82.58%
6345 Cell Phones	5,649.57	11,112.00	(5,462.43)	50.84%
6350 Travel & Ent	8,026.50		8,026.50	
6370 Meals	4,014.21	11,136.00	(7,121.79)	36.05%
6380 Travel	578.24	5,496.00	(4,917.76)	10.52%
Total 6350 Travel & Ent	$ 12,618.95	$ 16,632.00	$ (4,013.05)	75.87%
6390 Utilities			0.00	
6400 Gas and Electric	1,011.39	1,800.00	(788.61)	56.19%
6410 Water	2,038.62	1,200.00	838.62	169.89%
Total 6390 Utilities	$ 3,050.01	$ 3,000.00	$ 50.01	101.67%
6450 Contract Labor	12,224.49	2,400.00	9,824.49	509.35%
6470 Laboratory Fees	40.00	552.00	(512.00)	7.25%
6550 Office Supplies	29,893.88	22,140.00	7,753.88	135.02%
6630 Professional Development	1,500.00	24,480.00	(22,980.00)	6.13%
6680 Reference Materials	52.68	2,868.00	(2,815.32)	1.84%
6770 Supplies			0.00	
6780 Marketing	322.00		322.00	
6782 Pharmaceuticals / Injectibles	78,229.32	50,124.00	28,105.32	156.07%
6785 Medical	13,349.59	18,036.00	(4,686.41)	74.02%
Total 6770 Supplies	$ 91,900.91	$ 68,160.00	$ 23,740.91	134.83%
6786 Linens	831.30	5,400.00	(4,568.70)	15.39%
6790 Program Expenses	495.00	1,800.00	(1,305.00)	27.50%
6820 Taxes			0.00	
6840 Local	6,231.46		6,231.46	
6850 Property	2,779.89	1,968.00	811.89	141.25%
Total 6820 Taxes	$ 9,011.35	$ 1,968.00	$ 7,043.35	457.89%
9770 Guar Pmnts to Owners		616,674.00	(616,674.00)	0.00%
9780 Guar. Payment - Smith	122,523.09		122,523.09	
9800 Guar. Payment - Jones	165,950.95		165,950.95	
9810 Guar. Payment - Williams	151,394.75	16,121.00	135,273.75	939.12%
9820 Guar. Payment - Young	110,481.37		110,481.37	
Total 9770 Guar Pmnts to Owners	$ 550,350.16	$ 632,795.00	$ (82,444.84)	86.97%
Total Expenses	$ 3,097,072.50	$ 3,223,791.00	$ (126,718.50)	96.07%
Net Operating Income	$ 175,250.08	$ 265,310.00	$ (90,059.92)	66.05%

Figure 7 – **Budget to Actual P&L**

As you go through the budgeting process, you'll note that your two largest expenses are generally rent and staff. I usually recommend that groups think hard about maximizing the rent payments by having extended hours and possibly also weekend hours. You pay for the facility 7 x 24 x 365, so why not use it more fully than 9-5 Monday-Friday? This also goes to improving the patient experience. Busy people appreciate having some appointment times outside of normal working hours. Most groups don't attempt this, as they worry about being able to staff it. The groups who've done this successfully, however, find it's fairly easy to staff when people get some flexibility. Many clinic employees appreciate getting to work longer (perhaps four 10-hour days) and take a weekday off, so it's definitely worth exploring, as you'll be utilizing your facility far better than most.

With the staffing expense, it's good to mention that under-spending here may cost you more in the long run. Both understaffing and underpaying individuals can be costly mistakes, leaving you in that hard place of being "penny wise and pound foolish" with staff who are inefficient and ineffective. More on that in Chapter 10.

Since we're talking about financial analysis, I'd like to cover a few other related topics to help you with planning and decision making.

Cost of capital - This term gets tossed about a fair bit. Simply, it means that if you need to borrow money for a purchase or expenditure, how much interest will you have to pay? How much will it cost you to get access to that money? You can ascertain that by reading loan or equipment lease agreements for the terms. If those seem too long or complicated, please be sure you have your attorney or administrator review them for you and call out any questionable or troublesome clauses. Remember, the big print giveth and the small print taketh away. Be sure you've had a review of the small print! If it's not obvious, you may need to back into the interest rate. This means looking at it like an algebra problem and solving for X, which is the interest rate. If in doubt, ask the salesperson or the banker. If they cannot answer it simply for you, ask to see the calculation, and the amortization schedule of all payments.

Don't borrow until you know exactly what it is costing. This is true for leases on buildings that include the cost of tenant improvements too. Be sure to understand what interest rate the landlord is baking into your lease. It may be more cost effective for you to get a bank loan to finance tenant improvements yourself. If considering a big piece of equipment, it may be cheaper to get a bank loan to finance the purchase at a lower interest rate than the leasing company will charge.

Return on Investment (ROI) and **Break Even Analysis** – These terms are similar and frequently confused with one another. They seek to answer similar questions. When you make an investment in a new piece of equipment or a new service line, a **Return on Investment** calculation reveals the percentage you will you earn on your investment. For instance, if you invested $100,000 in something, and saw new revenue of $110,000 in the first year, you'd have a "**Return on Investment**" of 10%. Make sense?

Similarly, if you invested that $100,000 in January, and by November you had recouped the $100,000 in increased revenue, your break-even would be 11 months. So, the first seeks a numerical answer to how much money you'll make with a given investment, and the second tells you how much time it will take to recoup your initial investment.

Eligibility Verification - New Process Return on Investment Calculation		
Daily count of appointments		187.8
Total eligibility failures per day		31
Error rate		16.51%
Hard failures per month given 20 working days		620
Estimate of % that would have been fixed with existing workflow		48%
Reduced number of errors with new process		322.4
Average payment per claim	$	189.04
Total claims NOT denied with new process	$	60,946.50
Apply time value of money to A/R balance - this calculates how many claims would have been uncollectable given a first denial	$	51,103.64
Net increased monthly collections with new process	$	9,842.86
Cost of staff for new process	$	3,124.73
Return on investment - monthly	$	6,718.13
Return on investment - annually	$	80,617.55

Figure 8a – **Return on Investment** Calculation

	Break Even Calculation New Medical Equipment		
A	Initial Cost of Equipment Purchase	$ 78,000.00	
B	Average reimbursement per procedure	$ 234.00	
C	Cost per procedure	$ 75.00	
D	Net income per procedure	$ 159.00	(B - C)
E	# of procedures per month	80	
F	Income per month	$ 12,720.00	(D x E)
G	Break even at # of months	6.13	(A / F)

Figure 8b – **Break Even Calculation**

Real World Work – Budgets and Financial Tools:

1) Download last year's **Profit and Loss Statement** into Excel, and average the 12 months to get your monthly average.

2) Use this to set up a new budget for the current year if that hasn't been done already. If it has, thank your manager or bookkeeper. Lunch out would be nice too. They're doing a good job for you.

3) Analyze it for unusual items and adjust your budget for the current year.

4) Re-load your new budget into **QuickBooks**, or have your accounting folks load it into your system for future analysis.

5) When you have a month's worth of data, work through your variance analysis and research any items that exceed both thresholds. Make notes on those, and you're ready to present to your partners!

6) Pour yourself a nice celebratory beverage. That was hard work. Well done!

Chapter 4

<u>Assets</u>

Now for the real fun! Assets! This is the stuff you own. Think equipment, furniture and CASH! Yes, your cash is an asset – it is something you have, and it adds value to your business. It allows you to pay the bills, buy new equipment, and pay your team and yourself. It should always be flowing (we'll discuss more of that in a bit) and you should always know how much you have.

Some practices will have more than one bank account, and some have only a business checking account. For most groups, a business checking and perhaps a money market "Rainy Day" fund will do. It is wise to have 3-6 months of expenses for your business set aside as a cushion in a separate account, or to have those funds readily available to you in an active line of credit from your bank.

Some banks and accountants recommend having two separate accounts – one for receipts (where the money you earn gets deposited) and one for disbursements (where the money is spent from). The theory is that if your bank account information is compromised on the disbursement side (check washing or similar scams), then the bad guys can't get at ALL of your money, only what you transferred to that account when you paid bills. Given the improved banking security, and the advent of online bill pay, I generally don't believe this is necessary. If your practice brings in more than $5 million a year, you can certainly check in with your accountant and your banker to see what they recommend. In most cases, I see it adding more complexity than the practice needs, and it basically just provides more security for the bank (who insures your funds against theft due to bank fraud) and creates more work for you.

Please beware of fancy "cash management accounts" or other banking bells and whistles that some banks will try to sell you. Unless you have multiple millions of dollars flowing through your account in a given year, you will likely be just fine with simple business checking. You should expect to pay $30 – $50 per month to have that type of account, and it should include remote check capture and online banking. There is no need to pay hundreds of dollars per month for "overnight sweeps" or "analysis" or other nickel and dime charges for services you're not likely to use. One practice we worked with was paying their big name bank more than $900 per month for banking services that had been sold to them, but that they never used. They canceled those, and returned to simple business checking, saving more than $10,000 per year.

Your tax accountant will love me for this next one. Please be sure you have separate accounts for business and personal items. Separate credit cards too. Almost all business expenses can be deducted on your tax return, but most personal expenses cannot. We have run into several practices where there is a mixing of personal and business expenses. While mingling is good if you're at a cocktail party, it's not good with business and personal expenditures. Accountants call this type of hodge podge "co-mingling," and the IRS really frowns upon it. So, do yourself a favor, and keep 'em separated.

What should be separate, and what can I run through my business? Here is where I can give you some general guidelines, and then I'll strongly suggest that you clear whatever you're doing with your tax accountant. They're really smart about these things so you and I don't have to be. Like your patients look to you for advice on their health, you can look to your tax professional for advice on these types of things.

Depending on your practice's legal structure, you may be able to expense the cost of a leased vehicle, your mobile phone, and other items you use for yourself. There are expenses that are individual to you that are definitely work related, and therefore deductible – medical malpractice insurance for one – and those that are not, like your groceries. If you're not sure, ask! You can begin by asking your practice administrator, and if he or she is not 100% sure, then you can go to your accountant. Most group practices have a well-established system for handling practice and physician-specific expenses. It may be that you can run your own medical and dental insurance premiums through the company, and possibly also your flex plan. In some ownership structures, you cannot, so be sure to check with your tax professional.

The second asset we'll discuss is your **Accounts Receivable** or **A/R**. This represents all of the money that others owe to you for services you've provided for your patients. Basically, it's a big pile of money that you're waiting for, and it should be closely managed. If it's not, the pile shrinks, and even though you did all of the work, you might not get all of that money. We'll talk more about the management of **A/R** in later chapters, but for now, you should begin to think of it as something that has value and should be closely monitored. <u>It's your money, it just isn't here yet.</u>

I can't stress this part enough: most physicians have little or no idea what's going on with their **Accounts Receivable**, and yet, it's where ALL of their money is. We'll do a much deeper dive on this in Chapter 6. For now, understand that all of that **A/R** is an asset that you own.

Other Inventory is a third asset of your clinic. In some practices there are significant investments made in inventory that is going to be sold or dispensed to patients. If you have more than $1,000 per month of these types of items, you should have some kind of system to manage and track that inventory.

This may be books, videos, supplements, batteries, other small appliances, DME (braces, splints, etc.), shoes or sandals with good arch support, or other tangible things that you order and resell to your patients. Please note there are some things you order that you use in the course of treating patients that you will not bill them for – examples would be tongue depressors, exam table paper, and sutures. Those are disposable medical supplies and don't need to be tracked for reimbursement, as they are assumed to be part of the cost of the patient's visit. Someone needs to track the inventory of medical supplies so that you reorder in a timely fashion, but there isn't an income component to those items.

When you are reselling items to patients, you need to have a good pricing structure, and a good system to track inventory levels for reorder, and to know which patient purchased which item, and what they paid. **QuickBooks** includes an inventory module and there are other inventory management systems that include bar code or QR code technology that are far more sophisticated. Again, it's best to match your volume of sales with the level of sophistication you need in a system so that you don't "over buy." Whatever you use to track inventory, I always recommend recording sales to individual patients within your current **practice management** system for simplicity. That way, if a patient calls to ask about their bill, it's all in one place.

When you buy things to resell them to patients, most often, your accountant will want your finance person to record that expense in a category called **Cost of Goods Sold**. You will also want to track the income for that in its own category so that you can see if what you're selling is profitable, and if you should continue, or even expand the offering. As an example, if you purchase 10 bottles of supplements for $10 per bottle, and you sell them for $15 per bottle, your **Cost of Goods Sold** would be $100, and your income from supplement sales would be $150. When you net those two numbers, you're left with a profit of $50. This is a good thing, and you should do it again next month.

You should check the relationship between all of those numbers each month to make sure you are still turning a profit. If volumes are falling off, or if you're not profitable month over month, stop. Usually, having something like this available at the practice delights patients, so look for that feedback, and if it's working well, expand. This is something you can task one of your team with, and perhaps even give them a small percentage of the profits if they manage it well. Passive income streams are a good thing. In the past, physicians have shied away from "selling" anything over the front counter, but now it is becoming far more acceptable, and in many cases, expected, that you will have a bit of a retail component to your practice. Run it well, make it attractive, and have that win-win of something that delights your patients and that makes you a bit of a profit. They will appreciate that you have done the work of vetting the product so they can trust it will be high quality. Many patients will pay extra for that, rather than blindly ordering online.

When doing profitability analysis, be sure to account for hidden costs too. Does the retail portion take up a lot of space? If it's more than a shelf or two, you may want to allocate a portion of the rent cost. One of our clients has a sleep center that uses an entire room to display CPAP equipment for sale. It is quite profitable, and covers the rent cost on that square footage. If it didn't, they could reclaim it as an additional exam room. Be thinking that way! And, if the sales of products require a lot of time from your staff, be sure to account for that too. There are many good ways to add to your income, and it pays to be mindful of the whole cost so that you can be sure that they are truly profitable.

Real World Work – Assets:

1) Check out how much is in your bank account. If you don't know how or where to get this information, find out. Be sure that you or one of your partners has all banking login info and authority, which means full admin rights. Do NOT leave this solely in the hands of your spouse or one of your employees, no matter how much you trust them. It's not their business. It's yours.

2) Take a look through a couple months of your practice's bank statements. See where the money is coming from, and be sure you understand the sources. Also check the outflows and be sure you understand those too. You'll see big ones for rent, payroll and medical supplies. What are the others? Do you know all of the vendors you're paying? What is your average daily bank balance?

3) Run your **Aged Accounts Receivable** report. Check out the total outstanding, and as a simple exercise, multiply by 50%. The total is your **Gross Charges** still outstanding, and 50% of that is a VERY rough estimate of what you can expect to collect of that outstanding amount. That's an asset for you!

Chapter 5

The Dark Side – Embezzlers

You're thinking that you've heard some horror stories from other practices, but how often does this really happen? Unfortunately, the national statistic is that 83% of practices will suffer from some kind of embezzlement during the course of their history. And that's just a measure of the ones we know about! The very best thieves go completely undetected and then move on to victimize other practices. If you and four physician friends are together for a drink, chances are only one of you has NOT been embezzled. As a physician, you are especially susceptible to embezzlers for multiple reasons. You:

- Are likely very busy with patient care and don't have a lot of time for financial review
- Have a little experience with finances, but perhaps not enough to spot warning signs
- Trust your people, which is lovely, and scary
- Feel like you have much better things to do than set up **internal controls** (or you may be wondering what an "internal control" actually is)

So, how does embezzlement happen? For people who are inherently honest, it's hard to imagine how to successfully steal from someone else. We're just not wired that way. Believe me, there are many creative ways. One dishonest practice manager we know of over-ordered immunizations in her pediatric practice (which was typically a large expense) and then returned 10% of them and had the return refunded to her personal credit card. Then she went shopping for herself! No one caught the discrepancy between the 100% of immunizations she'd ordered and the 90% that the practice actually administered for quite a while. She made off with thousands of dollars over several years.

Another smart but crooked manager knew that her boss reviewed payroll, but that he only looked at the net pay amounts, and the practice total amounts. She used that knowledge to embezzle from the practice by inflating her salary, but then increasing her deductions, so her net pay was always correct. She filed for a huge tax refund at the end of each year, but was never detected by the owners of the practice. Many years and many hundreds of thousands of dollars later, this seemingly honest manager was caught by a routine payroll review.

There are many other stories, including one assistant manager who did the clinic's Costco shopping. She would load up the cart with things for herself, and then drop those off at home on her way back to the clinic. No one reviewed the receipt in detail, and she wasn't caught for several years. Many thousands of dollars of tax-free income for her... a big loss for the clinic.

As a last example, one of our client's front desk receptionists began pocketing cash from the sale of hearing aid batteries and other over-the-counter items. She began "kiting" to cover her theft. She would post a payment from another patient onto the account of the one who had bought the batteries, and then another to cover the second patient's transaction, frequently splitting cash, check and credit card transactions into multiple parts on different accounts. Her strategy was to make the money trail so difficult to follow that no one would be able to do it. When she was eventually caught and fired, her parting words were, "You'll never figure it out!" We estimated that she stole $15,000 – $30,000 over the span of just a few months.

Those are just a few of the horror stories we've heard and seen, which illustrate some of the more nuanced ways in which a clever thief will steal from their employer. Please don't assume that it won't happen to you. These are really smart people; if only they would use their powers for good.

Embezzlers come in all shapes and sizes. We've seen employees steal from their bosses, partners steal from one another, and even spouses who managed the practice steal from their spouse who was busy seeing patients. They may seem the most dedicated of all, when in fact, they're robbing you blind.

They take all kinds of money in all kinds of ways.

So, given all of this scariness, how do you protect yourself? There are several simple things you can do to set up **internal controls**, which are processes that make it difficult – if not impossible – for someone to steal from the clinic. Some of my favorites are:

- **Daily cash balancing**
- Balancing between bank deposits, **practice management**, and accounting systems
- **Bank account reconciliation**
- **Electronic Funds Transfer (EFT) payments**
- **Lockbox**
- Cash disbursement controls
- Adjustments review

Daily cash balancing is just that – each person who receives **payments** from patients at the clinic should have a cash drawer or box that they balance each day. The total they took in from all forms of payment should be "batched" and should match what they entered into the **practice management** system. ALL patients should be given a system-generated receipt for any payment made at the clinic. This mostly applies to front office folks.

Bank to **practice management** system to accounting system balancing should be performed daily (or weekly if your practice has less than $500,000 in annual revenue). This means simply matching the amount of money that came into your bank account with the amount that was posted into your **practice management** system (that would be reflected as a daily balance), and those two should be matched with what was posted into **QuickBooks** or whatever accounting system you're using. While there may be a few differences (timing differences by a day or two), the numbers should be very close, if not exactly matching. If they are not matching, ask more questions.

Each of the clinic's bank accounts should be reconciled each month by the manager or bookkeeper, and that should be made available to you for review. The reconciliation should balance to the penny (yes, I used to be an auditor, and yes, this is always possible), and the ending balance for last month should ALWAYS be the beginning balance for this month. No exceptions.

We encourage all of our clients to set up **payments** from insurance companies via **Electronic Funds Transfer (EFT)**. This means the insurance companies send your **payments** directly to your bank account, which safeguards the flow of cash. This eliminates one way that embezzlers can get their hands on the money – if it doesn't pass through their hands on the way in, it makes it tougher to steal. In most cases, you can get 80 – 90% of your **payments** coming in this way. A caveat here: some insurers are attempting to pay by sending a credit card number to you on a voucher. If you are receiving these, please have your staff call to STOP them. This just costs you an extra 2-4%, as you have to pay your credit card merchant service fees to collect the money. The insurers can pay you via **EFT**, and if for some reason, they cannot, then they can send you a nice, old-fashioned check.

If you receive a lot of checks even after transitioning as many as possible to **EFT**, consider utilizing a **lockbox** service. This is a special PO Box that is set up to receive your checks, and they are deposited directly into your bank account by a licensed, bonded, and insured person. This is the next best thing to **EFT payments**, as the money never makes it to the clinic. Be sure to check pricing on these – there are many different vendors who offer this (banks, billing companies, stand-alone **lockbox** companies) and be sure you're getting all and only what you need at a good price. You can compare this cost to your staff time to open mail, copy checks, and prepare bank deposits. The lockbox should scan all documents to a HIPAA secure location that you and your staff can access and that is easily searchable with multiple filters.

Having taken care to safeguard cash on the way in, let's talk about the ways that cash leaves your practice. It's likely that you have a payroll service, and you or one of your partners should have administrative access with logins to that so that you can review it at any time. You should review payroll reports with your manager prior to payroll being released. This should take 5-10 minutes max. If you have a lot of experience with and a high degree of trust in your manager, you can review this after payroll has been processed, but be sure to do it regularly. Get familiar with the reports and the "usual and customary" amounts for everyone.

As for other ways in which you spend money, you likely write checks, or use online bill pay, or have some expenses paid directly from your bank account (**Automated Clearing House or ACH** payments) or credit card. My strong suggestion is that one of the physician partners is the check signer (not the manager unless you have a large practice with other **internal controls** in place), and that a partner is the only one who can authorize and finalize online banking transactions. Each of these transactions should be accompanied by an invoice with appropriate detail so that you can see what you've spent and why. As for ACH transactions, you should review that section of the bank statement monthly – a quick scan should reveal a host of familiar transactions. If any are unfamiliar or excessive, investigate. Lastly, the same type of review should be done each month with the clinic's credit card statement. This takes just a few minutes each month and buys great peace of mind.

This last one is sneaky – an Adjustments Report is available through your **practice management** system, and shows what your billing team "wrote off". These should be reviewed for reasonability, and to spot any odd trends with specific payers, employees, or amounts. Be sure to ask questions so that you understand why things are being written off. If you're not satisfied with the answers, ask more questions. It's your money.

Now that we've been through several **internal controls**, you may be sighing and thinking, "This isn't for real. It won't happen to me. All of our people are trustworthy." I hope so! Recall that 83% of your colleagues probably had the same exact thoughts… just before they were embezzled.

How will you know? Red flags include employees who:

- Don't share their work
- Won't explain things to others
- Never take time off
- Won't delegate tasks
- "Lose" reports or fail to give you answers to questions
- "Forget" to follow up
- Tell you, "It's too complicated to explain"
- Won't give you logins to any system because it's "their work"
- Cannot answer questions about reports, numbers, discrepancies, even given time to research

If you see any of the above, please move on establishing **internal controls** immediately. If anyone who is involved in your practice has any hesitation about implementing these, keep pushing and keep asking questions. If you have concerns, or if things just aren't "adding up," spend some money by engaging a forensic accountant. If you uncover an embezzler, this can save you literally thousands. And if you find one, PROSECUTE! Most medical practices do not prosecute, as they are embarrassed and just want to fire the person and have the problem go away. This allows the embezzler to move on to another practice and steal from someone else. We see this time and again. Enough so that in our market there are 6-8 embezzlers who routinely apply for positions we have posted on behalf of our clients. We know who they are and can eliminate them in our search, but they continue to prey on other practices. They will recirculate as long as they go unprosecuted. Take the time to press charges and do your colleagues a favor by stopping them for good.

Real World Work – Embezzlers:

1) Pick two **internal controls** from the list to start with.

2) Check to see if they are already in place. If not, ask your manager to set them up. If there is any push back, have a different conversation.

3) When those are in place, pick two more and keep going.

4) When you've exhausted my list, check with your accountant for more.

5) When you reach a level of reasonable security, stop adding controls and just monitor. A few hours spent on this will buy you a great deal of peace of mind, and will keep the practice nicely safeguarded. Sometimes just having the **internal controls** in place and talking about them will deter a would-be thief.

Chapter 6

Practice Management Software and Reports

To round out our section on managing your money, we'll need to spend some time talking about your **Practice Management (PM) software**. There are many of these systems on the market today – most of them integrated into your Electronic Medical Record (EMR), but some that are stand alone and interfaced to your EMR. Regardless of its structure, your **Practice Management** system is used to register your patients, record their demographic information, schedule their appointments, create insurance claims, and track your **Accounts Receivable**.

This system, like any other is governed by the GIGO rule – Garbage In, Garbage Out. Best if everyone can be well trained, and if the clinic can have established and documented workflows for each process. Here are some workflows we like to see documented for our clients:

- New Patient Registration
- Verification of Eligibility and Benefits
- Collecting and Posting Copayments
- Processing of Incoming Mail and Digital Storage
- Basic Account Balance Queries from Patients
- Regular Balancing Procedures
- Running of Management Reports (Manager)
- Submitting Patient Charges to the billing team (Physicians/Providers)

Workflows are a great place to start – you can check with your manager if you are not certain if written workflows have been established. It does require some effort to create them and to maintain them, but they also make excellent training documents when you have new hires who need to learn your clinic's way of doing things. We find many practices installed their EMR and **PM** systems with little or no training or implementation support. This may have saved money at the outset, but is likely costing your group more than it should if you're lacking in efficient and well-documented systems. Software implementation is truly a "you get what you pay for" exercise. We frequently go into practices and recommend a re-implementation of their software so they can garner the benefits of having it in the first place. The software you use on a daily basis should not be a necessary evil, it should be your friend.

The work of serving the patient and collecting for the services begins when the patient first contacts the practice and they are registered into your system. If that is done well, it contributes to what we call a **"clean claim,"** which is one that goes all the way through and gets paid by the insurance company the first time. This is cause for celebration. And, it requires a LOT of things to go right.

Our team's benchmark for **clean claims** with any of our clients is 95%. Be sure to measure this and push your billing team to get there. This goal is not only possible, but achieving it greatly improves your cash flow. Don't take "we can't" or "that's impossible" for an answer. It is possible, and they should absolutely be able to do it. If your existing team just can't seem to get there, you may need new people.

So, you've been cooking along, and now you're beginning to wonder exactly how healthy your **Accounts Receivable** are… and are things well managed? It's always good to have a "checkup" on that, and at a minimum, you should review a couple of reports each month.

First is your monthly financial summary. Nearly every **practice management** software system has a version of this report, but none of them call it the same thing. The report shows one line for each month of the year, and the line begins with "**Beginning A/R Balance**" then adds "**Gross Charges**" and subtracts "**Payments**" and

"**Contractual Adjustments**" to come out to an "**Ending A/R Balance**." The numbers should add all the way across. Some systems show other details like "**Bad Debt**" or "**Non-Contractual Adjustments**," but for the most part, the big pieces are Charges, **Payments** and Adjustments. No matter what your software calls it, your monthly financial summary should look like this:

ACME Clinic Monthly Financial Summary

Total Practice

Month	Beginning A/R	Charges	Payments	Collectable Adjustments	Non-Collectable	Ending A/R
January, 2018	3,200,942.62	2,038,289.03	(662,758.85)	(32,029.63)	(1,482,872.85)	3,061,570.32
February, 2018	3,061,570.32	1,815,813.82	(480,535.81)	(10,348.69)	(1,059,646.23)	3,326,853.41
March, 2018	3,326,853.41	1,883,855.40	(636,430.16)	(5,050.36)	(1,348,689.30)	3,210,538.99
April, 2018	3,210,538.99	1,869,622.48	(717,657.90)	(26,502.90)	(1,708,112.97)	2,627,887.70
May, 2018	2,627,887.70	2,110,539.86	(726,108.58)	(36,535.89)	(1,605,028.38)	2,390,754.71
June, 2018	2,390,754.71	2,046,522.50	(667,731.73)	(14,162.96)	(1,054,739.30)	2,700,643.22
July, 2018	2,700,643.22	1,865,389.55	(621,812.81)	(28,846.50)	(1,448,774.91)	2,466,598.55
August, 2018	2,466,598.55	2,159,011.86	(583,520.62)	(30,011.99)	(1,214,808.30)	2,797,269.50
September, 2018	2,797,269.50	1,573,159.00	(570,360.74)	(16,828.16)	(1,351,273.32)	2,431,966.28
October, 2018	2,431,966.28	1,844,410.10	(639,003.01)	(25,404.81)	(1,310,787.89)	2,301,180.67
November, 2018	2,301,180.67	1,924,156.45	(563,457.00)	(38,559.01)	(1,137,623.46)	2,485,707.65
December, 2018	2,485,707.65	1,790,594.08	(530,107.24)	(3,345.63)	(1,098,590.17)	2,634,258.69
Totals		$22,941,374.13	$(7,399,484.45)	$(287,626.53)	$(15,820,947.08)	
January, 2019	2,634,258.69	2,227,355.04	(606,514.50)	(24,079.33)	(1,200,107.30)	3,030,912.60
February, 2019	3,030,912.60	1,942,561.47	(521,321.36)	(13,699.80)	(1,220,957.79)	3,217,495.12
March, 2019	3,217,495.12	2,189,958.79	(742,611.71)	(21,523.25)	(1,720,270.89)	2,923,048.06
April, 2019	2,923,048.06	2,537,495.40	(726,272.61)	(23,801.14)	(1,492,794.14)	3,217,675.57
May, 2019	3,217,675.57	2,433,394.61	(693,441.12)	(20,519.18)	(1,551,769.76)	3,385,340.12
June, 2019	3,385,340.12	2,147,051.23	(596,414.96)	(19,643.94)	(1,410,650.29)	3,505,682.16
July, 2019	3,505,682.16	2,158,543.87	(832,012.22)	(34,244.93)	(2,007,726.24)	2,770,242.64
August, 2019	2,770,242.64	2,176,474.69	(722,575.43)	(29,010.89)	(1,741,886.01)	2,453,245.00
September, 2019	2,453,245.00	2,355,257.38	(811,134.69)	(23,164.42)	(1,297,668.82)	2,676,534.45
October, 2019	2,676,534.45	2,577,701.92	(743,411.29)	(46,467.18)	(1,718,927.94)	2,745,423.96
November, 2019	2,745,423.96	2,239,879.31	(649,995.29)	(11,153.82)	(1,667,906.98)	2,678,554.82
December, 2019	2,678,554.82	2,142,383.25	(708,467.53)	(21,388.07)	(1,602,198.26)	2,488,884.21
Totals		$27,108,056.96	$(8,354,178.71)	$(266,388.31)	$(18,632,864.42)	
January, 2020	2,488,884.21	2,386,913.90	(657,284.71)	(17,349.39)	(1,278,601.67)	2,922,562.34
February, 2020	2,922,562.34	2,372,437.59	(636,166.20)	(13,649.39)	(1,351,225.77)	3,293,958.57
March, 2020	3,293,958.57	1,271,563.62	(694,233.04)	(23,376.11)	(1,458,445.75)	2,389,467.29
April, 2020	2,389,467.29	728,545.99	(594,009.76)	(12,528.36)	(1,355,025.19)	1,156,449.97
May, 2020	1,156,449.97	1,299,971.74	(484,687.86)	(4,579.97)	(617,016.37)	1,350,137.51
Totals		$8,059,432.84	$(3,066,381.57)	$(71,483.22)	$(6,060,314.75)	

Figure 9 – Monthly Financial Summary

Once you have this run for the prior year or two, you can look at the trends in each category month over month. If your system will render this graphically, I always recommend that. Looking at tabular data can be a bit challenging, but when it's graphed… a picture is worth a thousand words. If your system doesn't render it graphically, export it to Excel, at which point you (or your manager) can make the graph. Here's an example:

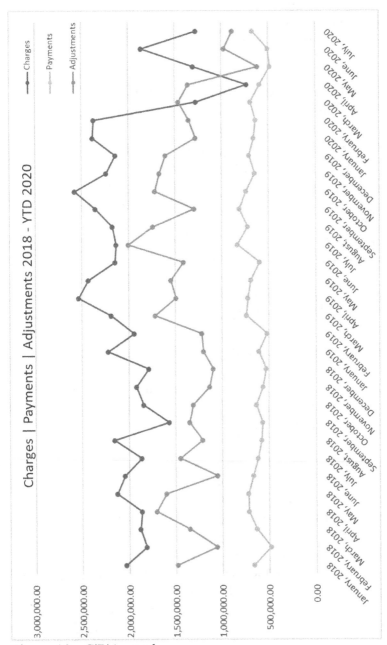

Figure 10 - C|P|A graph

As you can see, this is a great way to quickly evaluate the trends – you can even have Excel drop in a trend line. Is it headed in the right direction? (Up is usually good for Charges and **Payments**.) You can also easily see the relationship between the three big categories. If your **payments** are less than 50% of your **Gross Charges**, you may want to lower your **conversion factor** on your fee schedule.

If your **conversion factor** is $90 or less, you'll definitely want to do a deeper dive on the **contractual adjustments** that your billing team is writing off. They may be taking the easy way out and not doing the difficult work to follow up to get claims paid after they've been denied. We see this all too frequently. Physicians work hard to produce millions of dollars in **Gross Charges**, and then under-hire in their billing department, and hand the management and collection of ALL of those dollars to someone inexperienced, or someone who doesn't understand why it's important to follow up. Sometimes medical billers don't understand the impact of writing things off, and sometimes they just don't care. Frequently, they assume physicians are wealthy, so why should they work hard to make them even more money? If billing staff aren't managed, and if their work isn't reviewed closely, it's very easy for them to take write offs instead of doing the hard work. In some cases, we've seen poor software system set up where the system itself was automatically writing off anything that came in as denied or as a $0 payment, thus costing the practice hundreds of thousands of dollars in uncollected revenue. If you have that concern, ask your manager or a revenue cycle (billing) expert to look into your system for you to be sure this is not happening.

Once you've finished with trending your monthly financial summary, you'll also want to look at your **Aged Accounts Receivable** report. This shows your total **Accounts Receivable** (the money people owe you for services already rendered) divided into Insurance balances and Patient balances. The first is for claims that have gone out to insurance companies, but have not yet been collected. The latter is for bills that have gone out to patients on patient statements, but have not yet been collected. The report will also be split up at a high level by types of payers, so you should have categories for Commercial Insurance, Medicare, Medicaid, Motor Vehicle Accidents (MVA) and Workers Compensation (WC). This will be further divided into aging "buckets" usually labeled as follows: 0-30 days (or Current), 31-60 days, 61-90 days, 91-120 days, 121-150 days, 151-180 days and 180+ days. Some systems have fewer categories, so will top out at 90+ days or 120+ days, which is fine too.

This report is critical for you to see how well your whole group is doing at collecting money for services rendered. In general, you want to have lots of money in the 0-30 and 31-60-day buckets, and not much that's older. There are solid national benchmarks for this. Industry groups recommend targets for **Accounts Receivable Aging** as follows:

0-30 days at or above 70%
31-60 days at or below 10%
61-90 days at or below 5%
91-120 days at or below 4%
121-150 days at or below 3%
151-180 days at or below 3%
Over 180 days at or below 5%

Be sure to review your **A/R Aging report** monthly, and look for trends. Yours should look similar to the report shown in Figure 11a, and may also be displayed graphically by your **practice management** system, as shown in Figure 11b.

Aging by Financial Class

Financial Class		Deposit	0 - 30	31 - 60	61 - 90	91 - 120	120+	Total
Commercial	Patient	($604.24)	$20,864.23	$11,568.23	$5,267.90	$5,324.52	$38,241.61	$80,663.25
	%	(0.75)	25.87	14.34	6.53	6.60	47.41	68.55
	Insuranc	$0.00	$439,280.00	$78,222.38	$51,720.31	$7,469.85	$23,089.66	$699,782.20
	%	0.00	62.77	25.47	7.39	1.07	3.30	46.17
	Total	($604.24)	$460,144.23	$189,791.61	$56,988.21	$12,794.37	$61,331.27	$780,445.45
	%	(0.08)	58.96	24.32	7.30	1.64	7.86	47.79
Medicaid	Patient	($30.00)	$333.00	$0.00	$0.00	$0.00	$1,195.95	$1,498.95
	%	(2.00)	22.22	0.00	0.00	0.00	79.79	1.27
	Insuranc	$0.00	$135,256.42	$41,784.60	$842.00	$10,302.92	$15,783.80	$203,969.74
	%	0.00	66.31	20.49	0.41	5.05	7.74	13.46
	Total	($30.00)	$135,589.42	$41,784.60	$842.00	$10,302.92	$16,979.75	$205,468.69
	%	(0.01)	65.99	20.34	0.41	5.01	8.26	12.58
Medicare	Patient	($250.64)	$4,640.83	$1,001.87	$727.61	$73.98	$2,555.18	$8,748.83
	%	(2.86)	53.05	11.45	8.32	0.85	29.21	7.43
	Insuranc	$0.00	$411,903.72	$106,590.61	$8,805.75	$9,397.94	$7,809.24	$544,907.26
	%	0.00	75.59	19.63	1.62	1.72	1.43	35.95
	Total	($250.64)	$416,544.55	$107,992.48	$9,533.36	$9,471.92	$10,364.42	$553,656.09
	%	(0.05)	75.24	19.51	1.72	1.71	1.87	33.90
Military	Patient	$0.00	$1,153.38	$144.60	$27.70	$1.00	$53.04	$1,839.72
	%	0.00	82.26	7.86	1.51	0.05	8.32	1.56
	Insuranc	$0.00	$20,493.31	$26,960.00	$2,893.20	$1,445.00	$11,276.00	$63,067.51
	%	0.00	32.49	42.75	4.59	2.29	7.88	4.16
	Total	$0.00	$22,006.69	$27,104.60	$2,920.90	$1,446.00	$11,429.04	$64,907.23
	%	0.00	33.90	41.76	4.50	2.23	17.61	3.97
Motor Vehicle	Patient	$0.00	$0.00	$0.00	$0.00	$0.00	$0.00	$0.00
	%	0.00	0.00	0.00	0.00	0.00	0.00	0.00
	Insuranc	$0.00	$0.00	$0.00	$0.00	$453.00	$0.00	$453.00
	%	0.00	0.00	0.00	0.00	100.00	0.00	0.03
	Total	$0.00	$0.00	$0.00	$0.00	$453.00	$0.00	$453.00
	%	0.00	0.00	0.00	0.00	100.00	0.00	0.03
Self Pay	Patient	$35.00	$1,696.64	$2,692.65	$888.55	$1,958.35	$17,651.62	$24,922.81
	%	0.14	6.81	10.80	3.57	7.86	70.83	21.18
	Insuranc	$0.00	$0.00	$2,860.00	$0.00	$0.00	$0.00	$2,860.00
	%	0.00	0.00	100.00	0.00	0.00	0.00	0.19
	Total	$35.00	$1,696.64	$5,552.65	$888.55	$1,958.35	$17,651.62	$27,782.81
	%	0.13	6.11	19.99	3.20	7.05	63.53	1.70
Patient Total	%	*($849.88)*	*$29,048.08*	*$15,408.35*	*$6,911.76*	*$7,357.85*	*$59,797.40*	*$117,673.56*
		(0.72)	*24.69*	*13.09*	*5.87*	*6.25*	*50.82*	*7.20*
Insurance Total	%	*$0.00*	*$1,007,442.45*	*$356,817.59*	*$64,261.26*	*$29,068.71*	*$57,958.70*	*$1,515,548.71*
		0.00	*66.47*	*23.54*	*4.24*	*1.92*	*3.82*	*92.80*
Total	%	*($849.88)*	*$1,036,490.53*	*$372,225.94*	*$71,173.02*	*$36,426.56*	*$117,756.10*	*$1,633,222.27*
		(0.05)	*63.46*	*22.79*	*4.36*	*2.23*	*7.21*	

Figure 11a – **A/R Aging Report** by Financial Class

58

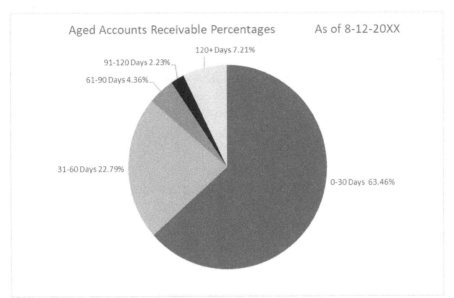

Figure 11b – **A/R Aging Report** Pie Graph

I find pictures are frequently easier to digest, and a pie graph works great for this analysis. If your **practice management** system doesn't generate it, you can export to Excel and create the pie graph that way.

One of the business metrics that is standard throughout the industry is the **Days in Accounts Receivable**. This calculation seeks to answer the business question: "How long does it take for you to collect the money you earned from the patients you saw today?" In highly performing practices, we'd expect to see that number in the 20-30 day range. Your number may be higher than that if you deliver OB services (**global periods** elongate the **Days in A/R**) or if you have a large number of surgeries, as insurance companies like to hold large claims or deny them for goofy reasons to see if your team will follow up. You may also have a higher number for **Days in A/R** if you have a lot of Workers Comp or Motor Vehicle Accident claims, as many of those go to litigation, and can take months or years to settle, and subsequently get paid. When they do settle, they generally pay pretty well, but there is a fair amount of paperwork. If you can handle the paperwork, and the long lead time on payment, both of those can be lucrative lines of business. Best to ease into it so that your commercial payers can help you fund the practice while you're filling the funnel with WC and MVA claims too. Gotta pay the bills along the way.

The **Days in A/R** calculation is as follows:

Total **Gross Charges** for 12 months divided by 365 = Average Charges Per Day.

Total **A/R** as of today divided by Average Charges Per Day = **Days in A/R**.

(Yes, this uses calendar days, not working days, which seems odd, but is the industry standard.)

Real World Work – **Practice Management** Software and Reports:

1) Print both reports as mentioned in this chapter.

2) Take a look at the graph for your Monthly Financial Summary (or create one if your system does not produce it that way) and note any trends. Investigate anything that makes you curious with your manager or the head of your revenue cycle team. For advanced groups, look at these items trended year over year, which will give you an idea of the seasonal variations in your practice. It will also inform your budgeting for upcoming years.

3) Look over your **Aged A/R** and see if you like the aging as compared to the benchmarks above. If you are meeting or exceeding these benchmarks, make sure it's not because your team is taking excessive adjustments. If everything checks out and your team is on the ball, take them all out for a nice lunch. They've earned it. If you're not there yet, begin to make a plan for how your group will work the old **A/R** and bring it back to a healthy state. You can hire this out as well, as there are Revenue Cycle Companies who specialize in helping to catch up on old **A/R**.

4) Run these two reports every month and review them with your partners and your revenue cycle team. Create performance targets including your **Days in A/R** and offer incentives to the team when they achieve them. One group gives out $100 to each billing staff person when they reach a goal. It's motivating and the manager loves walking around with $100 bills for everyone!

Section III

PLANNING

Financial, Strategic, and Retirement

How will you get there?

Chapter 7

<u>Strategic Planning</u>

As the old saw goes, "If you don't know where you're headed, any road will do." No book on running your business would be complete without some discussion of strategic planning. In fact, there are entire books written about just that. In the spirit of giving you the condensed version, my favorite statement about strategic planning is that it really boils down to answering three questions:
1. Who are we?
2. Who do we want to be?
3. How will we get there?

There are many consultants out there who do strategic planning for a living, and there are many ways to make it more complicated, but whatever your process, if you've answered those three questions, you've accomplished your planning.

I generally recommend setting aside a good block of time for this – a half day at minimum. Some groups make this a weekend affair at a lovely destination so that everyone is out of the "everyday grind" and can focus on thinking bigger thoughts. Some facilitators even collect cell phones at the door to be certain that everyone is present. This is about where you're going as a group, and about setting your direction. So, even if you're holed up in your office conference room for an afternoon, give it your full focus and undivided attention. Optimally, find someone outside of the group to take call so you are completely uninterrupted.

Who should attend? All owners/partners in the practice, your administrative and clinical leadership, and anyone else you consider crucial to the running of the business. There are frequently informal power brokers or "wise women" and "wise men" whom you may want to include. No hard and fast rules here – just think about who you'd like to have in the room thinking with you. Good thought partners will take you a long way.

I also highly encourage you to have this session facilitated by a professional. A good facilitator can keep things moving, ask probing questions, refocus the group when necessary, and will help you to produce excellent results. Best of all, they will take responsibility for recording everything and returning to you a complete written plan. This frees you up to just envision and think, and not worry about logistics. I've seen groups attempt to self-facilitate, or to use someone from within their team, and unless they've got years of experience facilitating, this is not a time to DIY. You're making a large investment in your future by devoting your time to this instead of seeing patients. Make sure you don't undermine that investment by under-spending on the facilitation.

When our group facilitates strategic planning, we typically begin with the creation or reaffirmation of the **Mission**, **Vision**, and **Values** for the group. Some already have some of those written, some have one or two, and some groups have none to start with. A set of quick definitions:

Mission – who you are... why you exist as an organization... your raison d'etre
Vision – who you will be... what you strive for... your end goal
Values – what you hold important on the journey to your **vision**... how you will behave

As an example, one group created this:

Mission
All of the physicians and staff at ACME Clinic are committed to:

- Comprehensive pulmonary care of the highest quality
- Excellence in clinical care, working relationships and business practices
- Creating inviting environments for patients and team alike
- Being members of the community at large
- Exceeding expectations

Vision
ACME Clinic will be the most comprehensive and convenient source of quality-driven care for all your pulmonary care needs

Values
- Joy
- Profitability
- Quality
- Patient Experience
- Reputation

Figure 12 – **Mission**, **Vision**, **Values** Example

If you don't yet have one, you don't need to reinvent the wheel. Ask your facilitator to send some examples ahead of your retreat to get the juices flowing. Google is also your friend... look for a few examples and begin to think about what's important to you. Borrow from other sources! You can derive inspiration from others and then tailor it to make it your own.

In the end, be sure what you have come up with resonates with you and the whole group. You can then publicize your **Mission**, **Vision**, and **Values** by including them on your website. You can also add them to your print materials, make them a part of your orientation packet for new hires, and you can even put them up on your wall. Our group has our **values** listed down the hallway to give everyone a daily reminder of *who* we are and *how* we are with each other on the path to fulfilling our **vision**.

This can be a long exercise, but it need not take up the whole retreat. If you're starting from scratch, plan to spend about an hour discussing and getting the high points, and then ask your facilitator to work with a few people on your team to wordsmith and bring back a final version sometime after the retreat. You don't need to get it perfect the first time.

If you're revisiting existing **Mission**, **Vision**, and **Values**, put them up on screen and invite open discussion about them. Do they still work? Have things shifted? Could some things be eliminated or enhanced? Does anything need to be added?

It's great to revisit them on a routine basis – perhaps annually or bi-annually – to be sure that as the landscape of your practice shifts, what you've stated about yourselves still resonates. Be sure to check in at a deep level, and not just rubber stamp it. This is the important stuff. Make sure that they don't end up as just words on the wall. Work hard and be intentional about incorporating your **Mission**, **Vision**, and **Values** into every aspect of your practice – hiring criteria, performance evaluations, decision making for the practice – everything.

Now for the planning itself. Once you're grounded in **Mission**, **Vision**, and **Values** for the group, it's time to start thinking about the future. We enjoy asking groups to envision where they'd like to be in five years. We spend a great deal of time on that – getting very clear about what it looks like. Any new locations? New partners? New lines of business? What will it take to support all of that? Will anyone retire in the interim? (More on this in subsequent chapters.) What will look the same and what will be different?

Industry groups sort the work of running a clinic or medical group into six separate segments, which are:

- Leadership & Organizational Governance
- Financial Management

- Patient Experience & Patient-Centered Care
- Clinical Quality & Risk Management
- Culture & Human Resource Management
- Technology

Once we've gotten clarity on what the organization looks like in five years, we talk about what would need to be in place two years from now in order to get to that five-year plan. This could be a bit challenging for the group if folks are not used to thinking this way, but with some time and a good facilitator, you can get there. Once you're clear about how things look two years from now, just divide that in half, and you have a one-year plan. What needs to be accomplished this year in order to get you to the two-year and five-year visions you've just created?

This should be made into an **Operational Plan** with accountabilities and due dates. In order for the strategic planning process to get any traction, your whole team needs to leave knowing that they've got their road map for the next year. We find quarterly check-ins to be invaluable in maintaining the momentum that is created at the retreat. If those aren't kept, it is easy to lose the momentum, and then the strategic planning just became a waste of time, money, and effort. Be sure to roll out the strategic plan to your staff upon return, especially to those who have accountabilities.

Yes, there are deadlines that won't be met. It's okay. Readjust and reassign. Check in with team members who are not meeting their accountabilities. If they are struggling, ask what it is that takes up their time. A good **Operational Plan** should help them focus on what's important. Here's an example from one of our clients:

ACME Clinic One Year Operational Plan - Finalized 8/27/20XX

Goal	Domain	Primary Accountable	Co-Accountable	Additional Resources	Additional Resources	Date Due	Notes
Define Day Rate by location	Financial Management	Mark		Sarah	Amy	5/1/20XX	18 patients per day is break even for the doc to get to bonus - will calculate for year end
Demonstrate ROI on PA hire	Financial Management	Amy		Jon		9/24/20XX	Not going to do this.
Analyze and review opportunity for Certified Professional Coder staff position	HR			Executive Committee		9/30/20XX	Done
Leadership team is scheduled for 3 meetings per year with reviews to discuss Ops Plan	HR	Jon		Matt		9/30/20XX	Dec XX, April, August, Dec XX
Review medical records release workflows	HR	Seth				9/30/20XX	All being sent via EMR (Jennifer processing now?)
Implement plan for ACME Clinic location #3: marketing, physician coverage, sub-lease	Operations Management	Sarah		Courtney		9/30/20XX	
Post signs in exam rooms welcoming New Patients	Patient-Centered Care	Jennifer	Mandy	Darla		5/1/20XX	Ordering frames
Identify quality metrics by disease state	Patient-Centered Care	Amy		Matt	Mark	5/1/20XX	
Schedule annual coding/chart review by auditor	Risk and Compliance Management	Jon				9/30/20XX	Done?
Ensure PCI compliance	Risk and Compliance Management	Matt		IT vendor		5/1/20XX	Amy giving vendor notice
Training and development plan launched for leadership team	HR	Darla		Jennifer		5/1/20XX	Initial meeting on 11/8/XX - like to attend MGMA next Fall
Increase Per Visit Value by 10% over previous 4 quarters	Financial Management	Physicians		Jon		5/1/20XX	Measured
Implement policy for responding to adverse events	Risk and Compliance Management	Amy		Executive Committee		5/1/20XX	
Implement regular reviews of Site Standards - 1x per year per location	Patient-Centered Care	Sarah				5/1/20XX	
Develop patient safety culture of empowerment, ownership and empathy	Risk and Compliance Management	Amy		Jennifer		5/1/20XX	Quarterly visit / field trip - how MA's can be comfortable asking doctors questions - next Staff Meeting
Identify referral sources and deepen relationships	Patient-Centered Care	Carla		Executive Committee		4/1/20XX	Jon to invite Carla to next EC
Implement Thank You notes and Starbucks cards for patients who frequently refer New Pts.	Patient-Centered Care	Mark				5/1/20XX	Next Doctors' Meeting agenda
Revise A/R and A/P processes - combine revenue to share overhead and define expense allocations - get rid of disbursement account	Financial Management	Mark				3/31/20XX	In process
Develop budget and review monthly and annually	Financial Management	Executive Committee		Jon		6/1/20XX	
Implement financial audit processes across organization	Financial Management	Mark		Leadership Team		6/1/20XX	
Employee incentive compensation plan identified and implemented	Financial Management	Jennifer		Sarah		12/31/20XX	Reviewed Dashboard and LT is working on incentive plans to implement and measure in January
Provider compensation plan review	HR	Executive Committee				10/1/20XX	Do we adjust the second tier %?
Ensure completion of IT Annual Security Risk Analysis	Operations Management	Amy		Darla		5/1/20XX	Amy to talk to IT vendor
Provider Employment Agreements updated and include performance expectations	Organizational Governance	Executive Committee				12/31/20XX	
Ensure facility licenses and accreditations are current	Risk and Compliance Management	Matt				12/31/20XX	
Standardize vendors across locations (medical and office supplies)	Financial Management	Seth	Mandy	Sarah	Tanya	3/31/20XX	70% complete as of 12/5/XX - will do audit of office supplies with GPO
Physician recruitment plan in place	Operations Management	Jon		Jennifer		1/31/20XX	
Ensure efficient operation of call and benefits centers	HR	Seth		Seth	Tanya	1/31/20XX	
Mission/Vision/Values developed and shared with employees and patients	Organizational Governance	Jennifer		Mandy A		5/1/20XX	Do signs for each clinic
Implement quarterly provider peer review	Operations Management	Executive Committee				5/31/20XX	Next Doctors' Meeting agenda - Matt to pull 2 charts notes from each provider and route to EC
Mission/Vision/Values posted on website and clinic lobbies, marketing materials, EE handbook	Organizational Governance	Jennifer		Leadership		5/31/20XX	Jon to email to Amy
Develop manuals, training, workflows by position	Organizational Governance	Jennifer		Leadership Team		5/1/20XX	Jon to email to Amy
Develop culture of continuous improvement: PDSA (Plan, Do, Study, Act)	Operations Management	Jennifer		Leadership		6/30/20XX	Big progress here!
Fully implement shared overhead plan	Financial Management	Jon		Darla	Leadership Team	6/30/20XX	DONE
Provider code of conduct written and implemented	Organizational Governance	Mark				DONE	

Figure 13 – Acme Clinic Ops Plan

We frequently run into groups who are great at visioning, and not so great at execution. We can all relate to the grid in Figure 14, originally developed by President Dwight Eisenhower. There is a seductiveness of spending all of your time in Quadrant 1. After all, that's where the fires are burning brightly, and where all of the cool firefighters are! Quadrant 3 is also attractive… so much urgency! We sometimes forget to check the level of importance because everything feels urgent. It must be dealt with now!

Quadrant 2 is where the good leaders spend their time. It's a long-term investment of time and energy in the direction of the organization, and it's the mission critical stuff.

	URGENT	NOT URGENT
IMPORTANT	**1** **DO** CRISES	**2** **PLAN** GOALS & STRATEGIC PLANS
NOT IMPORTANT	**3** **DELEGATE** INTERRUPTIONS	**4** **ELIMINATE** DISTRACTIONS

Figure 14 – Important/Urgent Grid (aka The Eisenhower Matrix)

This distinction frequently separates the managers from the leaders. The good managers address all of the urgent stuff. The good leaders address all of the important stuff, and in doing so, minimize the amount of stuff that becomes urgent. You may find that you have managers who seem to be stuck on the urgent stuff, and unable to get to the not urgent but important tasks. If you want to continue to have them function as managers, this may be fine. If you want to evolve them into more effective leaders, some coaching and development usually goes a long way. You may encourage them to delegate some of the urgent items (handling coverage for staff who are calling out, etc.) so they have more time to focus on what you've put into the **Operational Plan**. Be clear about your expectations, especially if their deadlines continue to slide. And, if they cannot make the transition to working on the more important long-term objectives, even with coaching, it may be that the role has outgrown them and it's time for a change. Maybe they need a new seat on the bus, or maybe it's time for a new bus.

This is a new skill set, and some won't rise to the occasion. That's okay. It's good to be clear about what the business needs and make necessary changes either through coaching, development, reassigning job duties, or outplacement. Remember, it's your business. It needs to work and everyone in it needs to work too. Holding onto an employee who is no longer a fit only adds unnecessary stress, expense and delay. More on critical conversations in Chapter 10 on the Human Resource.

Once the **Operational Plan** is underway, beware of adding new responsibilities and tasks onto your management and leadership team. The tendency is that new things will come up and one or two of the partners will instruct the management team to focus on that now, to the detriment of the **Operational Plan**. This risks putting your whole organization off track from your Strategic Plan.

This is the biggest pitfall we see with medical groups. Don't let the urgency of new things derail the work you've done to make a good plan! Keep track of new things that spring up and seem important – there will be many – and decide as a group where they fit into the **Operational Plan**. Add them in priority order, and reassign dates or accountabilities as necessary. It is incumbent on each member of the management team to assess whether their personal accountabilities and due dates (their "To-Do List") is doable. If not, they need to ask for dates to be pushed back or others to take on tasks so that their list is reasonable and achievable. Nothing is more dispiriting than a list that is so huge, you're set up for failure before you even begin. Make sure you've set your whole team up for success!

Now, go forth and execute on that beautiful Strategic Plan that you've created.

Real World Work – Strategic Planning:

1) Talk with your team and schedule a Strategic Planning retreat if it's been more than a year (or never) since your last one.

2) Ask around to get names of consultants or professional facilitators. Be sure they've done many strategic plans and ask for their general process in doing so. Get references too. Are they asked back to the same clients year after year?

3) Make an investment in your future. Budget for the retreat:
- Facilitator cost – expect $2,000 - $20,000 for facilitation depending on whom you hire and how long the retreat is
- Meeting expenses – food, lodging, meeting space, travel expense
- Opportunity cost – not being in clinic or the OR for that time.

4) Get to planning! Enjoy the process of finding some clarity about your future direction. Be prepared for some big things to come up. Some of them may be hard to hear, or hard to process. This means you're getting to the important stuff. Don't be shy. Lean in.

5) Communicate, communicate, communicate!

Chapter 8

<u>Financial Planning</u>

As a part of your Strategic Planning process, you'll undoubtedly come up with some new things that you want to do. Many will involve **Capital Asset Purchases** and long-term investments.

We define capital purchases as something that the owner expects to hold for more than a year, and is not bought or sold in the normal course of business. For a medical practice, this could include new diagnostic equipment, new furnishings or exam room equipment or even a new building.

In most cases, when a group wants to add something new, the first question is what will be the **Return on Investment (ROI)**? We've discussed that calculation earlier, and if it's not clear how to do it, hire this out. Any time you're contemplating spending more than $30,000 – $50,000 on anything, it's good to have a solid analysis. How long will it take for the investment to create a return? Or, said differently, how long before you recoup your initial investment? Purchases of equipment that have an **ROI** inside of a year are easy to justify. Those with a longer time horizon may take a sharper pencil.

Secondly, once the purchase has shown an acceptable **ROI**, your next question is where to get the money? You may have investments of your own to draw from. You may want a bank loan, or you may be able to get terms from a leasing company. Be sure to consider the **cost of capital** on each. If your investments are currently earning 8%, that's your cost of utilizing your own money. If you can get a bank loan for 5%, that's cheaper money. Or, if the leasing company is offering you a "capital lease," meaning you own the equipment at the end of the lease by paying $1 or some such terms, perhaps their interest rate is lower than the bank's. However, a standard lease may be a better alternative if the equipment is fragile or the technology is rapidly evolving. This allows you to effectively rent the equipment, rather than buying it, if you think you'll want to trade it in for a newer model within 2-3 years.

One thing is for certain, the salesperson who stands to make a tidy commission off of your purchase will ALWAYS tell you it's a great deal. Get an analysis from someone else – someone objective.

If you and your group are entertaining the notion of a new building, congratulations! I generally recommend physicians diversify their investments, and real estate is usually a good way to do that. It typically appreciates over the years (depending on the market) and it is nice to pay rent to yourself. This is an area where a good tax accountant and a good real estate attorney can be of assistance. Generally, we see building ownership set up separate from the practice ownership, and formed as a separate **Limited Liability Company,** or **LLC**. This works for new office buildings and new stand-alone surgery centers and diagnostic imaging centers. If developing either of the latter, engage a good consultant there too, as both have very different construction and regulatory requirements from your average medical or office building.

We see real estate investment as a part of a well-rounded strategy for physicians to build wealth and create a legacy. Again, no DIY here – an investment in using some smart consultants will pay hefty dividends.

As you're sailing into your high-income producing years, and you're considering other types of investments, tax planning becomes paramount. I cannot stress this enough. There are many different tax advantages for business owners, and this is an area that can get esoteric. Good to have a knowledgeable tour guide and advisor to make certain that you're getting full tax benefit from being a business owner. Otherwise, why take on the headaches? This could be your financial planner, tax advisor, or CPA, or a combination of all three.

The next bit of planning… you guessed it, retirement planning! Even if you're years away (or think you are), a little planning here goes a long way. How many more years do you plan to practice? Are their major life expenses (college educations, weddings, big trips) between you and retirement? What do you want your retirement to look like? All of these things can and should be addressed by a professional financial planner. This is another area that smart people can begin to figure out for themselves, but would likely be better served by engaging a professional.

One of the wealth management groups we know routinely works with groups of physicians to shelter $260,000 or more per year from income tax. This kind of magic is all legal, above-board, and can make an enormous difference in what your retirement years look like. A talented financial planner who is good with plan design can help you to avoid tax-related pitfalls, and overpaying taxes as well. Safe Harbor plans can be created or modified that allow you to shelter income and give your employees a nice matching benefit for their retirement. Again, there are entire books written on the subject – suffice to say that a little professional guidance in this area goes a long way. Now that you're running your business as best you can, and producing excellent financial results, you'll appreciate someone who is helping you to use those intelligently.

One of the other questions we routinely get about finances is how to protect them? There are so many types of insurance out on the market for business owners, the effect can be dizzying. Here is a short description of the most common products:

BOP or **Business Owners Policy** – protects you from employee theft, wrongful termination (to a minimal degree – see **EPLI** below) and other general business risks to the business owner. Expect to pay $500 – $5,000 per year depending on the size of your practice.

P&C or **Property & Casualty** or **General Liability** – this is routinely required by your landlord, and protects the practice and you from a lawsuit filed by someone who was injured while at the clinic. Commonly referred to as "slip and fall" coverage – it is routine for every business. Expect to pay a few thousand a year – again, depending on the size of your business. You'll want to have the certificate of liability available to provide copies to your landlord and potentially to any lender. You may need to list your landlord as an "additional insured." Your broker can handle that for you.

Med Mal or Medical Malpractice – many consider this a necessary evil for all physicians. I actually like to view the Med Mal carrier as a good partner in making sure practices are well run and systems are in place to ensure the best outcomes and patient safety. Many of the national companies have excellent training programs and other resources. If you haven't checked into this, take a moment to do so. Expect to pay between $10,000 – $100,000 per year depending on your sub-specialty. This is a good policy to put out for bid from time to time. The market is becoming more competitive, and with the evolution away from **tail coverage** on claims-made policies, it is easier to move between companies. If you have been employed by a large group or health system, you may have been covered by an **occurrence-based policy**. If that's the case, make sure you understand the difference between occurrence and claims-made policies. If not, consult your insurance broker.

Cyber Liability – this is a newer coverage with the rise of EMRs and all kinds of personal health information (PHI) being stored digitally by medical practices. The hackers are out there, and they're coming for your data. Be sure you have excellent (and annually tested) security on your IT, and be sure you have adequate coverage for **cyber liability**. Practices who are hacked face ransomware costs, and fines if their PHI is breached. Your med mal policy may include some **cyber liability** coverage, so check there first, and then add additional coverage as you deem necessary.

EPLI or **Employment Practices Liability Insurance** coverage – this protects you even further from wrongful termination or harassment lawsuits and provides for defense costs and settlements too. As our society becomes more litigious, these types of coverage come to the fore. Ask yourself some hard questions about how you conduct business and how you relate to your employees. Are good HR policies in place? Do you stick to them? Do you have a friendly environment, or are employees treated in a questionable way at times? Perhaps you feel good about your interactions, but one of your partners is a bit more aggressive or inappropriate? This kind of coverage is not required, but it may behoove you to carry some depending on your circumstance. Just be aware, as with embezzlers, there are opportunists out there looking to hire on with the intent to sue. Doctors are seen as deep pockets and easy targets.

In the end, insurance of any kind is about mitigating business risk, and every business owner will make different decisions depending on what keeps them awake at night. It would be cost prohibitive to buy enough insurance to mitigate every risk, so this is a pick and choose situation. A good insurance broker will be honest, and will not sell you coverage you don't need.

Real World Work – Financial Planning:

1)   Schedule a "checkup" with your tax accountants, financial planners, and insurance brokers. If you haven't done a deep dive with each of them in more than a year, it's high time.

2)   Discuss any big new investments with your partners and make some plans for who will take action steps to make those happen, including the above checkups.

3)   Don't hesitate to put things out for bid – good professionals will respect that. And, remember that the lower cost option may not always be the best value, it may just be the lowest cost. Caveat emptor.

Chapter 9

Succession Planning

So, with all of this planning, aren't we done? Nope. When you think really long term, and you want to retire, how will you do that? As entrepreneurs always ask: What is your exit strategy? For physicians, you can sunset the practice and close it down (my least favorite option), you can sell it to your partners (probably most common), or if you've hung out a single shingle, you can sell it to an incoming young doc who wants to take over the reins.

If you're thinking that you're on a 10-15 year time horizon until you retire, it's a good time to start thinking about the next generation of leaders and owners for your business. Maybe there's a young doctor who has joined in the last few years who seems to have what it takes to carry the responsibility of ownership. Never too soon to start grooming a budding new leader. As you've learned in reading through this book, there is an incredible amount to know, and an incredible amount of nuance in how to run a practice. And, with a constantly shifting landscape, it is great to identify your new up and comers. Obviously, if you're part of a group practice, this is a conversation to be had amongst all the partners.

If you're still 15-20 years from retiring, perhaps you want to look around to see whom you may want to add to your practice. More on adding partners in Chapter 12, but being strategic and selective about this is a must. Being clear about their trajectory is also a must. If you think someone is "partner material," tell them. If you think you'd like to sell the practice to them someday, tell them that too. (Don't announce your intention to marry someone the day before the wedding!) Many times, people don't see themselves as capable, but when someone else does, they begin to step into that role more and more, and they become a self-fulfilling prophecy.

Once you've chosen your heir apparent, and they've expressed interest, set aside some regular time to meet with them to share more about the business. This is a good time to execute a **non-disclosure agreement (NDA)**. If you are not familiar with these, consult with your attorney. Even with an **NDA** in place, these conversations require a great deal of trust, as you'll be pulling back the curtain so they can see the wizard. Be ready for that to feel a little uncomfortable, especially if you're used to being in charge, and being the only one privy to confidential information.

Check to see if there are a few duties you can share – perhaps some of the staff reviews or other minor points of running the business. Talk with them about what interests them, and what they naturally excel at. I've seen some physicians who gravitate to the finance work, and others who are wonderful in relating to the staff. Be sure to include them in any strategic planning, and be sure their voice is heard.

Lastly, this is not a transaction to attempt on your own. Buy-Sell agreements can be very complex, and you want to be sure you've structured it well, so that it is very clear what will happen and when, how the practice will be valued, and what your incoming owner will pay. A good attorney can be invaluable in this process. Again, this is something you'll do once in your entire career, so a small investment in hiring a professional can go a long way.

Real World Work – Succession Planning:

1) Look around – do you have an heir apparent or two?

2) If not, begin looking to recruit some. If so, open the conversation over lunch out or happy hour so that you have some time to discuss.

3) Once you've ascertained their interest, begin to formalize a plan with timelines and the buy-sell process.

4) If this book has been helpful, give them a copy.

5) Engage your practice attorney to help facilitate the transfer of ownership. Start that conversation early as well.

Section IV

PEOPLE

Staff, Extenders, and Partners

Who is going with you?

Chapter 10

Your Most Valuable Resource – The Human One

When we look at the finances of a medical practice, the largest expense is staff salaries. Said another way, the biggest investment you make every month is in your team. How do you know if you're "right-staffed?" How do you know if you have the right people in the right seats on the bus? And how do you know if you're paying them enough? Or too much?

All good questions. I'd encourage you first to honestly consider how you consider your staff. Are they your friends and family and you cannot imagine ever letting any of them go? Do some of them have "tenure?" (As in, they can't be fired – ever – and they know that?) Or, do you consider them minimally trained, necessary expenses who can be replaced with another minimally trained person if they leave? Or, are they a valuable and highly performing resource that always has your back?

If you resonated with either of the first two, consider that you will get what you expect. In the first case, the "family feel" may feel great in your clinic, but too much of a good thing can lead to entitlement, tenure, and the "untouchable" employee who can do no wrong. This is toxic. Likewise, the attitude that everyone is expendable and replaceable at a moment's notice and no one is truly valued for their work will likely result in poor quality work because they sense that you don't care about them.

We've seen clients with both cultures, and neither works well in the long run. In the "family feel" scenario, we frequently see ineffective and toxic employees running roughshod over the manager and even the physician owners, and for some reason, this behavior is tolerated. In the culture where employees don't feel valued, they won't do high value work, which is also quite costly.

When we think of performance metrics in relation to Human Resources, the most prevalent is the group's turnover rate. Said simply, what percentage of your employees left or were terminated last year for anything other than a life change? (Going back to school, moving out of the area, or having a baby are not considered "turnover," they are simply life changes and don't impact your numerator.)

Some groups have rampant turnover (>25% is considered quite high, while 10% is a bit more standard), and fail to understand the financial impact. One group we've worked with had a turnover rate of 65%, and yet they continued hiring at the low end of the pay scale and providing minimal training for their employees. The message from the get-go was, "We don't really value you," and, "You're easily replaceable," so they got marginal performance, which resulted in several terminations, more new hires, costly training, and the cycle continues. Until they change their fundamental culture and their attitude towards employees, they will continue to suffer from a financial and performance standpoint due to the high turnover.

In the US today, the cost of turnover is estimated to be between $15,000 – $85,000 per employee.

Just let that sink in for a moment.

Recent estimates are that in any given year, 25% of employees in the US will leave their job. Further, 77% of those departures are preventable if the employers respond to issues appropriately. To put it another way, let's assume that 25% of your patients come in with the same diagnosis and the treatment is very costly. Further, had those patients received some different intervention from you, 77% of the disease could have been prevented. In this case, the disease is called "turnover."

Now that you're getting a sense of the financial impact of turnover, consider the social impact too. If Sally the Medical Assistant is unhappy with the way she's been treated by the clinic, is she likely to be quiet about that? Usually not. She'll likely gripe to coworkers, you, your partners, her family, other friends at other clinics – anyone who will listen. Now you're experiencing social and reputational damage as well. That's more difficult to quantify, but there's a cost there too.

So, what are some things you can do to create harmony within the clinic, happy employees, and a highly performing team? Some of the most effective are:

- Get your Staff to Physician ratios right – don't understaff
- Don't underspend in terms of compensation
- Offer a healthy benefits package
- Include some performance-based incentive compensation
- Be mindful about the culture you're creating
- Celebrate and thank your team – frequently!

For years, we've seen Staff to Physician ratios in the 3:1 range. That was the gold standard until the MGMA came along and began doing their Cost & Productivity reporting. Something interesting came to light when they divided the clinics into "Average" and "Highly Performing." The Highly Performing clinics reported in with 5:1 or even 6:1 in places. This was cause for reflection. In digging a little deeper into those stats, even though those clinics clearly spent more on their salaries for staff, they had leveraged the staff and made the physicians so much more efficient that the payroll expense was more than covered with the additional revenue. (Recall my earlier comments about hiring Coders and Scribes, which are great examples.) While it seems counterintuitive, we see it time and again. Practices that invest in the care and feeding of their people reap the rewards.

With compensation, it's easy to fall into the trap of negotiating the lowest possible salary for a new employee. I've been down this path, and it doesn't turn out well. While you want to strive for relative parity amongst your clinic employees in the same roles, I find paying a new employee at least what they were earning at their prior job – preferably a bit more – is the best way to start. Many people tie their hourly rate or salary level to their sense of personal worth. We may not think that is a very healthy way to view one's worth as a person, but it's not likely something we're going to change. Be mindful of this as you negotiate, and as you give compensation increases over the years. For every $1 per hour of compensation you increase for an employee, it costs your practice $173 per month. From their perspective, $173 can make a huge difference. If someone is paid $18 per hour, they will have a monthly net pay of approximately $2,500, so that extra $173 can make a material difference in their life. For you as the owner, it will not have much impact at all. Be sure to keep this in balance, however. You need to pay yourself too!

If you're absolutely unsure what to offer someone, check with local and state medical group associations or staffing groups. Many will aggregate and publish salary surveys which will give you a good range within which to work. A good long-term goal for your practice will be to create standard job descriptions and wage ranges for each position. I generally recommend hiring in the top 25-30% of the area wage range. This will usually guarantee that you'll get the top 25-30% of the talent in the area. You can extrapolate to see who you will attract if you choose to pay in the lowest 25%.

My two favorite interview questions (and I tell everyone I interview that I always ask these same two questions) are as follows:
1. If you were offered the job, when would you be available to start?
2. If you were offered the job, what would you expect to be paid?

Their answer to the first question is telling. If they say they would need to give a minimum of two weeks' notice, this shows their professionalism and personal accountability to their former employer. If they are willing to "skip out" on a former employer, understand they will do the same to you when the time comes. It also shows a lack of personal accountability and integrity. Think twice.

The second question is a polite way to open the negotiations. I believe it is gauche to ask what someone is currently paid, although it is tremendously helpful to know the answer. Question number two almost always elicits a response that begins with, "What I'm currently earning is…" and then you can go from there. I typically respond to what they've said with, "That is well within our range." (Provided that it is!) We can then follow up with a second interview, after which we might have another interview, or we might call them with a job offer. A few more astute folks will negotiate their salary a bit (good for them!) and most will accept what's offered.

I ask these two questions at the end of every FIRST interview, so I know who I'm talking to, and if we're in the same universe in terms of compensation. If I'm interviewing for a position that I expect to pay $20 – $25 per hour, and the interviewee clearly wants $30 – $40 per hour, we shouldn't waste any more time talking.

It is necessary to let your team know that you value them. One good way to do that is to make sure you're paying them fairly and giving appropriate – and regular – compensation increases. I typically recommend an annual increase in compensation that is based on your metro area's **Cost of Living Adjustment (COLA)** (Google it for your area – usually around 3%), and the individual's contribution to the organization as a whole. Your "Steady-Eddies" should receive 2-4% increases each year, and your superstars should receive 5-10% or more, depending on the year, and the degree of their contribution.

We go into many groups who do not have the basic building blocks in place. Please be sure you have written job descriptions for everyone on the team, and that you have annual compensation increases and wage ranges in place. Without these, it is easy for high caliber team members to become discouraged and disenfranchised.

Benefits are something that are often overlooked as well. Do you offer major medical insurance for your employees? If not, why not? You are running a medical clinic. Shouldn't that be a given? Same with dental coverage. If you're serious about caring for others as a profession, I'll invite you to start with those closest to you and create a generous benefits package. Our group includes life insurance and AD&D as well. You may find that excessive – I find it part of what a caring employer provides, and those last two are pretty inexpensive. Lastly, make it easy for your employees to save for their retirements – perhaps consider a match. If you've selected the right people and you treat them well, they will return the favor! I have provided a very rich benefits package for my employees over the years and have never once regretted it. We have a very high-performance team and almost nonexistent turnover.

As you move to shift your culture to one of high performance, setting some goals with some incentive compensation attached is a great way to "catch 'em being good!" One of our clients struggled to get much past 85 new patients in a month. The administrator came up with a simple system – $100 for 100 – which he shared with the team. In any month where they exceeded 100 new patients, everyone on the team would get $100. Guess what happened the following month? You got it. 100+ new patients. AND, this continued for EVERY month thereafter! The clinic continues to grow, and now they are at $250 for 250. Still making it every month.

When you do the math, that kind of growth brings so much revenue to the clinic that the incentive comp paid out becomes a drop in the bucket.

So, incentive compensation does not have to be a big, complicated, scary thing. It can be as easy as $100 for 100. Just put it out there, measure it, and be sure to pay up!

As another example of shifting culture, one of our clients created a Performance Dashboard – shown here:

ACME Clinic Performance Dashboard

Area	Accountable	Measure	Baseline	Target	Current Performance	Definition
Call Center	Sally	% of Patients registered correctly	75%	90%	77%	Clean eligibility (clean claim?)
Front Desk	Margie	% of copays collected	67%	85%	73%	Out of total copays to collect, what % got collected?
	Margie	% of visits set up for card on file with pre auth	71%	85%	78%	Out of total visits that could have patient balance, what % got set up for credit card on file with pre auth to process
	Margie	% of insurance cards scanned & entered correctly	82%	85%	87%	Out of total visits, what % have updated insurance card scanned and entered into EMR
Human Resources	Abby	Retention %	65%	85%	67%	What % of employees were employed six months ago
Clinical	Mandy	Vascular Screening	57%	90%	68%	What % of patients have vascular screening completed?
	Mandy	Cycle Time - Diabetic Shoes	23 days	14 days	21 days	How long does it take for patients to have diabetic shoes from date of order?
	Mandy	% DME from Vendor X	76%	95%	88%	What percentage of DME is ordered from the vendor who is part of our buying group?

Figure 15 – Clinic Performance Dashboard

As you can see, the measures are mostly simple. A few of them take the revenue cycle team a bit of digging, but as they've put compensation on each of these, they have everyone's attention and focus. It is also a good idea for you and your partners to have some deliberate conversation about the culture you have and what you want to create. If you want to maintain the status quo as you're happy with it, great! If there are some areas you could improve, have at it. Most groups let culture happen accidentally, without being mindful about it. Some good questions to discuss: do we want a formal or informal culture? If we want to be a high-performance culture, how will we define that? How do we embed high quality health care into everything we do? Again, entire books have been written on the topic, but those questions will get you started.

Lastly, as a means of creating happy teams, celebrate them frequently and thank them in different ways. When was the last time you had a party at the office? Or offsite? If that's not your forte, ask your team to create a Fun Committee and put them to work figuring out quarterly celebrations. Everyone loves a party! Mix it up... maybe a potluck in the office one quarter, and happy hour out for another. Summer picnic in the park or someone's backyard, and maybe a fun sporting outing (bowling or mini-golf) so you can have some silliness together too. Give them a budget and smile when they spend it. Your team takes a lot of guff from patients. I've seen it play out many, many times where the patient is completely snarky at the front desk, only marginally better to the MA, and sweet as can be when they see you in the exam room. You can thank your team in myriad ways, and if it's not second nature for you to express your thanks, give yourself a recurring calendar reminder. Even doughnuts or fresh fruit one morning with a big THANK YOU note from you can go a long way. Have fun with it. Remember, people love to be appreciated.

No chapter on Human Resources would be complete without visiting the now famous question – Do you have the right people in the right seats on the bus?

There is no absolute right or wrong on this question, although I find that envisioning an old-fashioned scale (like the balance beam style that Lady Justice holds) in thinking about a team member. On one side of the scale is the work product that person produces. On the other side of the scale is the amount of organizational energy and effort that is expended to keep them happy within the organization. (Whether that is from you, or from your manager.)

Mostly, we look for team members where the scale is out of balance in favor of the amount of work product they generate. It can be out of balance the other way for a short time, but not for long, or you run the risk of angering other team members if you're constantly giving time and attention to someone who isn't producing much. Give some thought to this. If there are folks who are out of balance, start having that conversation, openly, kindly and authentically. We generally think of conversations like that on a continuum:

Coaching → Counseling → Disciplining → Termination

Coaching is just that – encouraging them to do a bit better, giving them new tools, and perhaps some additional training. Nothing need be documented – you should be having these conversations all the time. If the coaching isn't sticking and the person continues to underperform, it's time to move to Counseling. At this point, the conversations get a bit more serious, and you may want to make a quick note to their HR file with the date and the content of the conversation. I find that sharing the above continuum with them sometimes helps, explaining that we've been in "coaching mode" and now we're moving into a bit more serious zone. If their performance continues to lag, it's time for Disciplining. Those conversations need to be written and signed by you and the employee. Copies go in the HR file, and there are only two discipline conversations before Termination.

Having tough conversations if you don't have the right people is never easy, but it is one of the best things you can do as a leader. If they're underperforming, they know it at some level and need help figuring out what to do. I like to talk about the notion of creating smooth landings, and freeing people to find a position that is a better fit for them.

One of our consultants told me, "We don't fire people; they fire themselves. We just fill out the paperwork." I agree wholeheartedly. If we've been through the Coaching and Counseling, we've given them every opportunity to improve and keep their job. If they choose not to, they're choosing not to work here anymore.

In a perfect world, in thinking about leadership roles, the Coaching and Counseling should be the job of the manager. When an employee needs Discipline, having a physician present and participating can bring more gravity to the conversation. It is always advisable to have the manager in the room also, and to speak off of the written Discipline form so that you stay on track and cover everything that needs to be said.

If you are Terminating an employee, a minimum of two clinic leaders need to be in the room, ideally the manager and a physician partner or other senior leader. Decide ahead of time who will say what, and generally, the less said, the better. Be sure to have their final paycheck in hand, and be sure to get any clinic property they have, including keys, phones, laptops, etc. Then wish them well in their next chapter and know that you have done the hard work of strategic pruning when it comes to creating and maintaining a high-performance team.

Real World Work – Human Resources:

1) Calculate your group's turnover for the past year. If 10% or less, congratulate yourself! If >10%, get to work on this list right away.

2) Consider your group's prevailing attitude towards staff. Need some course corrections there? If so, discuss with your partners.

3) Take a look at your compensation across the board. It's good to graph this so you can see where everyone is relative to one another. Has everyone's compensation level been reviewed within the last year? Is it fair, given years of experience and level of contribution to the clinic? If not, make adjustments – pay raises only, not cuts, which are horribly demoralizing.

4) If it's been more than three months since your last celebration, schedule one.

5) Discuss culture and performance with your partners and choose some actions to measure and drive toward high performance.

Chapter 11

Extenders

I am frequently asked by clients if they should add mid-level or advanced practice providers into their group. And while there are some subspecialties for whom this makes perfect sense (surgical assists come to mind). I believe most physicians can benefit from an extender if they are reaching capacity in their practice. One of the metrics I like to use is that we ought to be able to offer a new patient an appointment with the practice within 2-3 weeks. Traditionally, many physicians held a long appointment wait as a badge of honor: "I'm so good you can't even get in to see me for six months!" As we move to a consumer-driven society, this kind of schedule management is not impressive, nor is it something to be proud of. Rather, the consumer-driven patient will just move on to the next physician, and you will have lost that business. Seen through their lens: "That doctor has such poorly managed scheduling that they cannot accommodate me for six months? I can't wait that long; I don't care how good they are." You've just flunked the patient's first impression of you.

If you're out that far, it would be good to know whether your partners are as well. If so, it's time to think about adding another clinician to the team. Does it make sense to add another physician or a mid-level? Consider your call rotation. If another physician would make life measurably easier in terms of your call, perhaps that's the way to go. If your partners are doing okay, but you're overwhelmed with work, a mid-level as an extender for you may be the answer. Be sure to vet them carefully to assure you keep up the quality of your practice. Ask about prior experience and get references.

This is a big investment, and a prudent business owner would calculate a – you guessed it – **Return on Investment!** In adding this new person to your practice, you're going to invest a significant amount in recruiting costs, orientation and training and salary until they are up to speed. Work with your manager to calculate all of the costs, and where their break-even number of patient visits will be. That is most clearly stated in terms of number of patient visits per day. You can easily calculate your average reimbursement per visit across your practice. Take 90% of that for a mid-level provider, as you're likely to have them doing 99213s and 99214s and other follow-ups, which don't carry as high a value. You may also need to adjust depending on the insurance contracts in your market. Many plans reimburse mid-level providers at only 85-90%. I suggest spreading the up-front costs out over the year, so it looks something like this:

	Return on Investment for a Mid-level or Advanced Practice Practitioner		
A	Annual salary	$ 130,000.00	Per contract
B	Annual cost of benefits	$ 26,000.00	Per practice data
C	Recruitment Costs	$ 15,000.00	Actual paid
D	Total cost of Provider Year 1	$ 171,000.00	(A + B + C)
E	Anticipated Visits Month 1	40	
	Anticipated Visits Month 2	60	
	Anticipated Visits Month 3	80	
	Anticipated Visits Month 4	100	
	Anticipated Visits Month 5	120	
	Anticipated Visits Month 6	140	
	Anticipated Visits Month 7	160	
	Anticipated Visits Month 8	180	
	Anticipated Visits Month 9	200	
	Anticipated Visits Month 10	240	
	Anticipated Visits Month 11	300	
	Anticipated Visits Month 12	360	
F	Year 1 Anticipated Visits	1980	Sum all E
G	Average Reimbursement Per Visit	$ 175.00	Per practice data
H	Times 90% for Mid-level payment	90%	National Average
I	Total Anticipated Revenue Year 1	$ 311,850.00	(F x G x H)
J	Return on Investment Year 1	$ 140,850.00	(I - D)

Figure 16 – **ROI** on Mid-level

As you can see, the calculation need not be complicated. The hardest part is making sure that you've captured all of the costs.

Once this is done, do the "gut check" and be real about whether you can fill up their practice. When you're coming from a place of overwhelm, it's easy to imagine that you're working at 150% of your capacity, and that you could easily hand off a third of your patients. It may be that you're only working at 120% and only a sixth of your patients could be considered "overflow" and ready to hand over. Be sure to check the data carefully with your manager so that you're dealing with real numbers, not just your emotions around working too hard. That way you can trust your **ROI** when you make assumptions about how quickly the new practitioner's panel will fill. As the owner of the business, this expense likely comes out of your pocket, so you'll want to be sure you don't alleviate stress on the work side, and then create a bunch on the financial side when that person doesn't cover their cost for many months longer than anticipated, and you're forking over a lot of your own take-home pay.

You'll also want to think about whether they will always remain in the role of an extender to you, or if they will begin to develop their own panel. Some states allow NP's and PA's to function fairly autonomously, and it is good to be clear about that up front as a part of the hiring process so there are no surprises down the road. Be clear about call responsibilities too – many groups use mid-levels as the "front line defense" and that should be made clear, along with any additional compensation you will pay to cover those duties.

Whatever your decisions above, you'll want to be sure you have an **Employment Agreement** prepared for them. It is great to have this mirror the physicians' **employment agreements** as much as possible for standardization and parity. Your **Employment Agreement** should address Term and Termination, Compensation, Notice required to leave, Responsibilities and many other basic terms. This is a great time to have a review and some assistance from your practice attorney. I generally suggest that mid-levels are treated like physicians in terms of a minimum 90 day notice to leave, as recruiting to replace them and credentialing and contracting timelines mean that a replacement will not likely be in place for 4-6 months in a best case scenario. Treating your mid-levels like executives in your practice is a great idea. They can be effective leaders too, and you should look for opportunities to promote their involvement, within the scope of their licensure.

Real World Work – Extenders:

1) Ask your front desk when the next available new patient appointment is. If more than 3 weeks across the board, begin the work to add another partner or a mid-level.

2) Determine if another physician is warranted, or if a mid-level is the right addition.

3) Complete the **ROI** carefully, with good data so you know what to expect.

4) Update and rework your **Employment Agreement** as necessary for this new hire.

5) Get to recruiting. Expect this to take many months, so start early!

Chapter 12

<u>Partnership</u>

Most medical groups are structured legally as partnerships, and when a physician has been working as a part of the group for an agreed upon number of years, generally they are eligible for partnership. This means being added legally to the ownership of the group. Becoming a partner carries risk in that now you are liable (in part) for the actions of the whole group, and it also carries reward in that it generally means you get to share in the profits at the end of the day. This is a big commitment for both parties, and as such it is generally recommended that the doctor work with the group for 2-4 years before partnership is considered. You want to date for a while before you get married.

Now, a little bit about risk and reward. Whether you are being invited to join as a new partner, or whether you are already part of a partnership that is adding a new member, risk and reward should always be commensurate. Consider as a young physician, you are being offered partnership in your group. One of the senior physicians, who is an excellent surgeon and clinician has a reputation for being a "ladies' man" and you've heard that he hits on the nurses at the hospital and the ASC. He isn't as smooth as he thinks he is, and his advances are generally unwelcome. You figure he's pretty harmless and is just socially unaware, however, no one in the partnership has spoken with him about this, and the behavior continues unchecked.

Consider if that is risk you're willing to take on. In a best-case scenario, he's a bit of a laughingstock, and the practice's reputation suffers a little. In a worst-case scenario, several of the nurses band together and file a sexual harassment suit naming him and including your entire group. Now, let's assume the profit share of becoming a partner adds 5% to your annual take home. This may not be a good balance of risk and reward. If the profit share adds 50% to your annual take home, that may be risk you want to bear. Everyone's risk tolerance is different, as is everyone's individual situation, so seek out good counsel from friends, family, and business advisors. In the final analysis, you need to be able to sleep at night with the choice you make.

In my many years of working with physicians, I have noted that the amount of stress you generally take on is considerable. Every time you meet with a patient, that patient brings their fears, anxieties, pain and suffering to that encounter. After taking on all of that stress throughout the day, many doctors have constructive outlets for all of that, like rock climbing, running marathons, making music, or cooking. Many have destructive outlets like gambling, using recreational or prescription drugs, kicking the dog, drinking to excess, or abusing their spouse or children. We are all human. In my thirty years in the industry, I've encountered physicians who have made each of the above choices. Know that you are considering entering a group of people who are human, and all of whom have weaknesses to go along with the strength required to be a successful physician. Know who you are getting "married" to before you sign partnership paperwork. Like you and me, all are human; none are perfect. At the end of the day, you need to be comfortable walking with – and associating with – your new partners.

If you are being offered partnership, and the group looks good (hopefully having none of the above issues!) you can use the knowledge gleaned in the first few chapters of this book and conduct your own review of the financials. If you have not been made privy to the financial reports of the group, now is a good time to request them. Make an appointment to sit down with the manager, bookkeeper, or managing physician partner to review them in detail. Make certain all of your questions are answered to your satisfaction. If they don't have all of the answers at their fingertips, make a follow up appointment, and continue meeting and talking until you understand ALL of the financial underpinnings. Look back at least two or three years. Ask for this year's budget too. You're about to buy into this entity, and as a possible investor, you NEED to see everything you want to see. If anything is withheld or if anyone is evasive, continue asking questions. If answers are still not forthcoming, think hard about whether this is the group for you.

Many businesses use debt to finance buildings, equipment, and in some cases, ongoing operations during growth phases. Ask for a schedule of the group's outstanding debt and its repayment. This should include long-term financing, short-term loans, lines of credit, and credit cards. Find out if you'll be asked to assume some of that or add your name to a personal guarantee. Be sure that you understand clearly what you are guaranteeing if you are signing on. Some banks require **unrestricted personal guarantees**, meaning that if the group of four physicians is adding you as a partner, and you sign an **unrestricted personal guarantee** on $500,000 of debt, you may be fully liable if the clinic defaults and the other four partners vanish. The bank could then go after your personal assets to recoup their funds. This may be a difficult scenario to envision, but it's not out of the realm of possibility. PLEASE understand exactly what you're signing, and if you are not well versed with partnership agreements in general, this is a great time to engage an attorney or business consultant.

A caution: Several years ago, my attorney taught me that lawyers can be sorted into two categories with regard to reviewing a deal. The first group sees their role as needing to point out everything that could possibly go wrong and seeks to guard against every risk imaginable. This tends to break deals, not make them. The other type of attorneys act as collaborators, mitigating reasonable risk while working in the spirit of getting the deal done. Deal breaker or deal maker? Make sure you have the type you want.

You'll also want to take a look at the group's performance as compared to the MGMA benchmarking data discussed earlier. Is there a culture of accountability and performance? Are key metrics tracked and published? Does the group have professional, high-caliber management in place? Look for some of these hallmarks of a well-run business. If they're absent, talk with your potential new partners about their willingness to move in that direction.

You'll want to be very clear about how the partners share expenses and profits. Have the manager or managing partner run through a sample month for you using your last month's productivity stats. Let them show you how revenue, expenses and profits would be allocated to you. Now is time for another gut check: does it all seem fair and reasonable? Some groups have formulas that favor the senior partners, resembling a pyramid scheme. If that's the case, can you live with it until you become a senior partner yourself, or is it time to respectfully request a change in structure? Again, spend some time here and be sure you understand this thoroughly. The biggest conflicts we see amongst partners comes down to – you guessed it – money.

Now, let's fast-forward several years, and assume that you are the managing partner (or one of the senior partners) and you are contemplating adding another partner. The first question I always ask is: Do they have "Owner DNA?" What I mean by this is, do they fully understand what it means to be an owner, and do they share the work ethic of the existing partners?

It is time for some very candid conversations about the "Give" and the "Get" for all of the partners. What do they Give to the organization? Hard work, long hours, commitment to attend Board Meetings after hours, assumption of risk for debt and overall performance of the organization, responsibility for leading and overseeing the group, and perhaps some sleepless nights when things aren't going smoothly. What do they Get? A seat at the table, a share of the profits, a sense of accomplishment, and the ability to build a legacy that makes a positive impact on the health of the community.

For some, that will ring true, and they'll be ready to sign up! For some, that may not seem like a good trade off, and if that's the case, it's your responsibility to help them see that they may not be a fit for the partnership. Some physicians are really great "employed physicians" and should stay that way. They are not cut out to be partners, and shouldn't be forced into it. The trick is in helping them see this for themselves, and creating a construct so they don't feel like second-class citizens, but rather, valued, highly-performing members of the team who are simply on a different track. Both are valuable to the group. The risk is in having one who isn't in the right category.

I've referred to "profit sharing" several times – it is important to note that this may come as part of a formal Profit Sharing Plan, which is formally documented and filed with the IRS, and has very strict and specific guidelines. We typically see these in larger, well-established groups. When we talk about profit sharing (lower case), this can mean splitting up the profits at the end of the month or quarter, or distribution of income from ancillary services. If you're distributing income from ancillaries, be sure you're on the right side of the Stark and Anti-Kickback legislation. This is a great time to work with your practice attorney to assure that your distribution formula meets those regulations. If it does not, the penalties are stiff, and can wipe out years of profit. Ignorance of the law is not a reasonable defense for a well-educated person. And you are.

Real World Work – Partnership:

1) If you're being invited into a partnership, do your due diligence! Request reports and schedule meetings and make sure that you understand who you are partnering with, and how the business has been run. Partnership can seem sexy and seductive from the outside…

2) If you're offering partnership to a young associate, have the authentic conversations about Owner DNA, and what it takes to succeed. Many have a glossy version of partnership in their head (see #1 above), and lack a realistic understanding of the hard work involved. Beware the Gen X tendency to write off all millennials as unfit for ownership – many are fit, and just need some coaching.

3) When figuring out your profit share, ensure that it is fair to all concerned and that you are in compliance with state and federal regulations. If you're now a senior partner in a comp formula that has unfairly favored senior partners to the detriment of junior ones, consider evolving that more towards the center. Again, a small investment with your practice attorney will alleviate a great deal of business risk here.

Section V

WRAPPING IT ALL UP

Did you get where you needed to be?

Chapter 13

<u>Miscellany</u>

In the process of writing this book I've come across several "aha's!" and realized that I needed a chapter on Miscellany. Or, if you're a Jeopardy! fan, "Potpourri." Here goes:

<u>Collecting Money from Patients</u>
Three thoughts here: First of all, make it as easy as possible for patients to pay you what they owe. There are many **Advanced Payment Mechanisms** on the market – be sure your practice has several of these in place. A patient portal is key so that patients can pay their bill online, and if you want to make it even easier for them, send an e-statement to them so they can pay from their phone. Easy peasy. Our Revenue Cycle Management (RCM) division highly recommends a card on file program with a credit card vaulting feature, so that your staff can get a form of payment on file (or activated and awaiting the Explanation of Benefits which will show the patient's responsibility) so that patient balances can be easily and quickly settled to their credit card. This can save your team hours in the collections run around, and it saves on statement printing and mailing costs, and best of all, it gets you paid within days, rather than months.

Secondly, we are one of the last industries that allows its customers to pay a LONG TIME after the service is rendered. In some cases, many months, by which time the patient may forget why they owe you anything, and your bill falls to the bottom of the pile. Many patients also expect their doctor to make them short term loans. They do this by requesting payment plans to pay for high balances. My firm recommendation is NOT to do this. You are not a bank. You did not go into business to make loans to patients. They can get the funds elsewhere, and pay you ON TIME. Many RCM professionals will read this and shake their heads and tell me I'm unreasonable. So… if you're so inclined, payment plans can be made as a LAST resort, and in no event for longer than three months. Again, with the "you are not a bank" thing.

Lastly, every practice will have some patients who don't pay their bills. Some assume that their insurance should have covered everything, and that it's your fault that you did something that wasn't covered. (I know, I know.) Some assume you are rich and don't need their money because the insurance already paid for most of it. Some are truly unable to pay.

My recommendation to physicians is to be compassionate with the last group – we've all likely been there at one time or another and we can relate. With folks who are choosing not to pay your bill, I recommend having your RCM team send three statements and make one outbound phone call. Industry knowledge tells us that if a patient hasn't responded by then, they're not likely to without a different type of intervention. With our RCM clients, we run those patient names past the physician for approval to move them to a pre-collect program. This sends a letter from a national collection agency stating that they owe a debt and if they do not pay, it may affect their credit rating. Please note, this stage does NOT impact their credit score, but it is highly effective at getting patients to pay.

For the small percentage who are remaining after this step, I recommend sending them to collections. They have received a service from you, and they owe you for a portion of that. They have a responsibility to make some arrangement for that. All that being said, I encourage each physician to reflect and develop their own personal philosophy about collections. Some of our RCM clients don't ever send patients to collections. Some send everyone with an outstanding balance over $100 after the above interventions have failed to elicit payment. Some send a subset after the physician reviews the list once more. I encourage each group to come up with a standard for the whole group to follow. I encourage each business owner to value their time and expertise, and I respect each business owner's right to make a personal decision about their collections philosophy. There is no wrong answer here. Just be consistent.

Tracking Performance

We've touched on performance-based cultures, and we've seen an example dashboard. Why are these important? The old saw says, "You get what you measure." So, from the earlier example, if you want more new patients, put the focus on more new patients. I can assure you that the month before the "$100 for 100" program was implemented, very few (if any) of the employees at that clinic knew how many new patients they had at any given time in the month. And, the month after it was implemented, EVERY one of them could tell you what their progress was toward that goal! It's true: You get what you measure.

Financial metrics are easy to track – some of my favorites are:
- % of copays collected out of total possible for the day/week/month
- % of patients with a form of payment on file and a credit card vaulted
- # of new patients
- coding distributions for new and established patient visits

Quality metrics can be fun too. Your health plan contracts may stipulate some, or if you are a medical home, there is certainly a long list. Some common ones:
- % of diabetics with a HbA1c in the last six months
- % of patients receiving a flu shot
- % of patients with no post-op complications

How about some patient experience metrics? I love these:
- Time to next available new patient appointment
- Time to answer incoming calls
- Abandonment rate of incoming calls on hold
- Wait time in reception area, in exam room, or total throughput time
- % of patients with complaints about their bill

Again, whatever you decide to track, first establish your baseline performance as of today, and then create goals that are a bit of a stretch, but reasonably attainable. Put these on graphs (a picture is worth a thousand words!) and hang them in the break room, or somewhere where your team can see them. Update them weekly with notes of encouragement and sit back and wait for the results. They will astound you. If you put some money on it ($100?), they will astound you even further.

Keep it simple, easy to track, and make sure your goals are around things that your staff can impact directly. Check in with them to see what they think of it. Congratulate them when they achieve a goal and get their assistance in setting the next goal. Watch your culture of performance blossom.

Esoteric Accounting Stuff Worth Knowing
There are two areas of accounting that are a bit more advanced, and where I see physicians (and other non-finance professionals) get hung up. The first is in the notion of Cash vs. Accrual accounting. Most small to medium-sized groups use Cash Basis Accounting, which means that cash is recognized and booked into the accounting system when it is received. So, if you saw 400 patients in January, and got paid $58,000 for that work, but the money didn't come in from insurance companies until February, the income would be recognized in February, NOT January. That's when the cash arrived in the bank account, and that's when it's entered into the accounting system and recognized as income. Similarly, if you paid medical malpractice premiums of $9,000 for the first quarter of the year in February, that expense would be recognized and booked in February, because that's when the cash left the bank account.

Larger groups will use Accrual accounting, which attempts to spread income and expenses over the appropriate time period. In the above example in an accrual system, the $58,000 in revenue created in January would be booked in January instead of February. It would be booked when created, not when the cash actually came in. This is an attempt to smooth the financials. With the medical malpractice premium, $3,000 of expense would be booked into each of January, February and March, as that's the time period that the expense was covering. Again, this acts to smooth the financials and lets you have a

112

picture that matches expense to revenue created in the period, not reflective of when it was actually received or paid. This accounting method is much more sophisticated, and I generally don't recommend it for groups of less than 20 or 25 physicians. It requires members of your executive team who are financial experts, and who can manage cash flow separate and apart from these statements.

If you're unsure as to which method your group uses, ask. This will give you great insight into what you're reading.

The second sticky wicket I've run into is where a group has short or long-term debt which creates what we call "Phantom Profits" at the end of the year. Even the name sounds weird, but when you hear this, understand that it is legit. It's a bit odd, and I'll do my best to explain.

When a group files their taxes, they utilize the information off of the **Profit and Loss statement**, which shows the income that came in, and the expenses that went out. If your group's **gross revenue** was $5,000,000, and your expenses were $3,500,000, according to the **P&L**, you generated $1,500,000 that was distributed to the partners as **net income**. Let's say there are five partners, so each has a distribution of $300,000.

Let's also assume that the group had some debt on a new piece of equipment that was placed into service two years ago and originally cost $500,000 and was on a five-year repayment schedule. So, this year, you paid $100,000 in debt payments and roughly $30,000 in interest expense.

Here's the esoteric part: the IRS considers the interest expense of $30,000 to be an expense incurred this year. You had to pay the lender for use of the money, so that's booked on the **Profit and Loss**. If you had chosen not to add this new asset, your group would have had a **bottom-line net income** of $1,530,000. Make sense?

Now, the principal of the loan is not an expense. It is a **Balance Sheet** account in the form of an asset you added two years ago, and a liability you created then. So, the principal payments of $100,000 this year came out of your cash, but are not recorded as an expense. So, the cash available for distribution to the partners isn't $1,500,000 as shown on your **P&L**, but $1,400,000 given the $100,000 in debt payments. Now, each of the partners gets $280,000 in cash, but pays taxes on $300,000. Voila. Phantom Profits.

You didn't pay taxes on the money when you purchased the asset, but you get to pay the taxes now. Oh joy.

If that's all still clear as mud, ask your accountant for an explanation. Perhaps share this example with them and see if they can build on it until you get a good understanding. Please rest assured, you're not alone – even some finance folks struggle with this one.

To DIY or not to DIY

At several junctures throughout this book, I have encouraged you to hire things out. Many physicians prefer the Do-It-Yourself route, and this is natural – medical school teaches you to be radically independent! It does not teach you to be in partnership with others, however. While going the DIY route can be initially less expensive, it can cost a great deal in the long run. Please don't assume that you have to figure this all out on your own… even if you are holding this amazing resource in your hands that seems to give you all of the magical answers. I can assure you that it doesn't!

Yes, I am a consultant by trade, so it's easy for me to say, "Hire it out!" as I stand to benefit. However, I can attest to the value of good thought partners. I use several in the running of my own business. Some urge caution, others say things about my growth and development that give me a stomach ache… and then I go out and do them anyway, like doubling the size of our consulting group, or writing a book. Some help me with specific areas of expertise, and in some cases I can return the favor. Some are friends and colleagues with whom I discuss things over coffee or a glass of wine, and others are friends and colleagues whom I hire formally because I need many hours of their expertise and I want to be sure to value it beyond a casual conversation. All of them are delighted to be asked and are happy to share what they know.

Make sure you have a great stable of thought partners. If your group seems a bit small, reach out to some folks whom you would consider good mentors and invite them for coffee or a beer. Let them know that you respect them, and that you're working on some things and would love their input. Make this a two-way street. If there is expertise you have that you can share, do that freely. It's great to have a focus on learning – think: see one, do one, teach one. You'll be amazed at the powerful group of thought partners you can create.

Real World Work – Miscellany:

1) Make sure your practice employs several different payment mechanisms. If you don't have at least three, add some.

2) Check in on your payment plan and collections policies and be sure they are consistently applied and that they match your personal philosophy. Value your time here.

3) Check to see if your group uses Cash or Accrual accounting.

4) If you've seen or heard of some Phantom Profits within your group, be sure that you understand it.

5) Use paid professionals well – not too much and not too little, and don't fall into the trap of feeling like you need to figure everything out on your own. If your list of thought partners seems short, make an effort to reach out to a new colleague or mentor whom you admire and open a conversation.

Chapter 14

Bringing It All Home

I've talked throughout this book about developing your internal team for high performance. In the last chapter, I talked a bit about building an external team of experts as well.

Here's a list of your core team. These are professionals you'll need on an ongoing basis:
1. Banker
2. Wealth/Financial advisor
3. CPA
4. Bookkeeper – not your spouse, please, unless he or she has a business that takes on other bookkeeping clients, and even then, that's a bit close to home
5. Attorney
6. Business consultant

Each of these folks should be intimately familiar with your business, and these should be long-term relationships for you. You should be able to contact them with questions at any time, and you may want to invite them to your board meetings from time to time so they know all of your partners too.

And now for your ancillary team – these are professionals you need on an episodic basis when something special is going on:

1. For new office space or remodel:
   a. Real Estate Broker

b. Architect
c. Contractor

For ALL three of these, please be sure they have a SPECIALTY in medical space and buildouts. Get references from multiple medical clients. This is an area where professionals will say, "Oh yeah, we've done medical before," but it is not an area they can dabble in. Either they specialize, or they don't. Don't skimp here – we've seen that move cost our clients thousands of dollars. And if the building you're moving into has an "in-house" architect who does not specialize in medical, insist on your own.

2. For other specialized services:
    a. Medical Scribes – you may want to consider an external scribe service – there are many good companies and scribes are a difficult position to train, with (expected) historically high turnover rates since many scribes are medical students on their way to residency
    b. Revenue Cycle (outsourced) and/or Collections Agency – if you've not had a Revenue Cycle Review by an objective outside third party in more than a year, it's time to do that, or be sure you are internally benchmarking to MGMA and that your team is performing at or above the 90th percentile
    c. Pension Plan Administrator – lots of complex laws here – this is definitely NOT a DIY situation
    d. Lab, X-ray, or other ancillary services – sometimes it makes sense for a clinic to do this in-house, and sometimes it makes sense to outsource it, but keep the services onsite at your clinic for your patients' convenience. Many companies will embed an employee at your location to capture your business. This requires yet another **ROI**.

As we come to the end of our journey together, I encourage you to review the results of your learning. I'm very hopeful that you found many pearls of wisdom along the way.

I'd encourage you to reflect on the hardest lesson you came across, or maybe any parts of the book where you shuddered a bit. Go spend some time there. Figure out whatever is weighing on you and create some concrete action steps. Believe me, you'll feel better when you're done.

Next, reflect on the best thing you got from this. What was the crown jewel for you? If there is an action item around that, make time to take care of it, so you garner the most benefit from reading this book.

Take a look at your Real World Work from the end of each chapter (also compiled for you in the following pages with time estimates). Have you completed it all? If so, revisit and see where you could go deeper, or share this book with someone else in your group as a way to mentor them and bring them along.

And now, I want to congratulate you on your leadership and on the tenacity it took to hang in with this all the way through 'til the end. For many of you, these concepts will be foreign or only slightly familiar, so this is true exercise for the brain. And, it can be tiring, so give yourself a bit of grace if your Real World Work list seems to go on forever. This is a journey, and your successful practice is the destination, so I'm glad to see you on your way!

My fervent hope is that this book has improved your practice in some measurable way and has given you increased confidence in how to run your business. Again, this book does not have all of the answers, but hopefully some good vectors for you to use as you find your way.

Please come back to this resource again and again, and please know that you are welcome to reach out to me with comments, questions, suggestions, or success stories sharing how you used it, so I can congratulate you.

To your success!

Jill Arena, FACMPE
jka@healtheps.com

And they all lived happily ever after with wildly successful practices.

TABLE OF REAL WORLD WORK

Section I: Data

Chapter 1 – Overview of Your Practice Finances	Time Estimate
1) Log in to your accounting system yourself – if you can't remember your login, get it refreshed and put it in your password vault. If you don't have one, get one assigned for you so you'll have it in the future. If you work in a large group that has an accounting department, request a copy and find out who you are to contact in the future when you want reports. SPECIAL NOTE for private practices: Verify that you or one of your physician partners is the Master Administrator on the account – this function should ALWAYS be held by an owner, NEVER an employee, EVEN if that person is your spouse. This keeps you in control of your financial data whenever there is turnover in employees, and there will be. I've had groups locked out of their own financial data, and needing to recreate months or years' worth of data because a disgruntled employee left and refused to give them access. If you don't do anything else as a product of reading this book, PLEASE do this one thing.	30 minutes
2) Run the **Balance Sheet** as of the end of last month – this can be found under Reports in **QuickBooks**, and you can enter the date you want to see.	10 minutes

3) Run the **Profit and Loss statement** as of the end of last month – also found under Reports in **QuickBooks**, and you'll need to enter a date range (usually last month or year-to-date).	10 minutes
4) Review them and begin to note any questions. Discuss with the person in your practice who has responsibility for the finance function. If they discourage you in any way from doing this review, find a new finance person. (See Chapter 5 on Embezzlers.)	40 minutes
Practice Finances Overview Total	**1.5 hours**

Chapter 2 – Profit and Loss	Time Estimate
1) Get ahold of your coding data. Look at how you've coded 99201-99205 and 99212-99215 over the past year. If your usage graphs peak at 201 or 213, you likely have room to improve your coding. Find a coder to help!	30 minutes
2) Take the next step with getting a scribe. If you've not considered it, begin your research. If you've researched, reach out to a scribe company, or post an ad yourself and start the hiring process. If you have a scribe that isn't working so well, check yourself and your feedback, and fix that, or get a new scribe. If you have a fabulous scribe, take him or her out for a nice lunch and say, "thanks, you're doing a great job!"	60 minutes
3) Find your insurance contracts. Set up a matrix like the one shown in Figure 5, and if you have **RBRVS years** that are more than a year or two back in time, get those babies renegotiated. Every day that you wait is costing you money that you deserve to be paid. If you are hesitating at all about doing this yourself, hire it out. Now.	12 hours
[I realize this is a lot. Don't quit now! This is BIG real work. It will take time. It will pay dividends. I promise. Do it for your own financial wellness.]	
Profit and Loss Total	**13.5 hours**

Section II: Money

Chapter 3 – Budgets and Financial Tools	Time Estimate
1) Download last year's **Profit and Loss Statement** into Excel, and average the 12 months to get your monthly average.	30 minutes
2) Use this to set up a new budget for the current year if that hasn't been done already. If it has, thank your manager or bookkeeper. Lunch out would be nice too. They're doing a good job for you.	60 minutes
3) Analyze it for unusual items and adjust your budget for the current year.	30 minutes
4) Re-load your new budget into **QuickBooks**, or have your accounting folks load it into your system for future analysis.	60 minutes
5) When you have a month's worth of data, work through your variance analysis and research any items that exceed both thresholds. Make notes on those, and you're ready to present to your partners!	60 minutes
6) Pour yourself a nice celebratory beverage. That was hard work. Well done!	
Budgets and Financial Tools Total	**4 hours**

Chapter 4 – Assets	Time Estimate
1) Check out how much is in your bank account. If you don't know how or where to get this information, find out. Be sure that you or one of your partners has all banking login info and authority, which means full admin rights. Do NOT leave this solely in the hands of your spouse or one of your employees, no matter how much you trust them. It's not their business. It's yours.	60 minutes
2) Take a look through a couple months of your practice's bank statements. See where the money is coming from, and be sure you understand the sources. Also check the outflows and be sure you understand those too. You'll see big ones for rent, payroll and medical supplies. What are the others? Do you know all of the vendors you're paying? What is your average daily bank balance?	30 minutes
3) Run your **Aged Accounts Receivable** report. Check out the total outstanding, and as a simple exercise, multiply by 50%. The total is your **Gross Charges** still outstanding, and 50% of that is a VERY rough estimate of what you can expect to collect of that outstanding amount. That's an asset for you!	30 minutes
Assets Total	**2 hours**

Chapter 5 – Embezzlers	Time Estimate
1) Pick two **internal controls** from the list to start with.	10 minutes
2) Check to see if they are already in place. If not, ask your manager to set them up. If there is any push back, have a different conversation.	20 minutes
3) When those are in place, pick two more and keep going.	10 minutes
4) When you've exhausted my list, check with your accountant for more.	20 minutes
5) When you reach a level of reasonable security, stop adding controls and just monitor. A few hours spent on this will buy you a great deal of peace of mind, and will keep the practice nicely safeguarded. Sometimes just having the **internal controls** in place and talking about them will deter a would-be thief.	30 minutes
Embezzlers Total	**1.5 hours**

Chapter 6 – Practice Management Software and Reports	Time Estimate
1) Print both reports as mentioned in this chapter.	10 minutes
2) Take a look at the graph for your Monthly Financial Summary (or create one if your system does not produce it that way) and note any trends. Investigate anything that makes you curious with your manager or the head of your revenue cycle team. For advanced groups, look at these items trended year over year, which will give you an idea of the seasonal variations in your practice. It will also inform your budgeting for upcoming years.	20 minutes
3) Look over your **Aged A/R** and see if you like the aging as compared to the benchmarks above. If you are meeting or exceeding these benchmarks, make sure it's not because your team is taking excessive adjustments. If everything checks out and your team is on the ball, take them all out for a nice lunch. They've earned it. If you're not there yet, begin to make a plan for how your group will work the old **A/R** and bring it back to a healthy state. You can hire this out as well, as there are Revenue Cycle Companies who specialize in helping to catch up on old **A/R**.	60 minutes
4) Run these two reports every month and review them with your partners and your revenue cycle team. Create performance targets including your **Days in A/R** and offer incentives to the team when they achieve them. One group gives out $100 to each billing staff person when they reach a goal. It's motivating and the manager loves walking around	60 minutes

with $100 bills for everyone!	
Practice Management Software and Reports Total	**2.5 hours**

Section III: Planning

Chapter 7 – Strategic Planning	Time Estimate
1) Talk with your team and schedule a Strategic Planning retreat if it's been more than a year (or never) since your last one.	30 minutes
2) Ask around to get names of consultants or professional facilitators. Be sure they've done many strategic plans and ask for their general process in doing so. Get references too. Are they asked back to the same clients year after year?	60 minutes
3) Make an investment in your future. Budget for the retreat: - Facilitator cost – expect $2,000 - $20,000 for facilitation depending on whom you hire and how long the retreat is - Meeting expenses – food, lodging, meeting space, travel expense - Opportunity cost – not being in clinic or the OR for that time.	30 minutes
4) Get to planning! Enjoy the process of finding some clarity about your future direction. Be prepared for some big things to come up. Some of them may be hard to hear, or hard to process. This means you're getting to the important stuff. Don't be shy. Lean in.	1-2 days
5) Communicate, communicate, communicate!	All the time

Strategic Planning Total	2hours + 1-2 days

Chapter 8 – Financial Planning	Time Estimate
1) Schedule a "checkup" with your tax accountants, financial planners, and insurance brokers. If you haven't done a deep dive with each of them in more than a year, it's high time.	3 hours
2) Discuss any big new investments with your partners and make some plans for who will take action steps to make those happen, including the above checkups.	60 minutes
3) Don't hesitate to put things out for bid – good professionals will respect that. And, remember that the lower cost option may not always be the best value, it may just be the lowest cost. Caveat emptor.	2 hours
Financial Planning Total	**6 hours**

Chapter 9 – Succession Planning	Time Estimate
1) Look around – do you have an heir apparent or two?	30 minutes
2) If not, begin looking to recruit some. If so, open the conversation over lunch out or happy hour so that you have some time to discuss.	2 hours
3) Once you've ascertained their interest, begin to formalize a plan with timelines and the buy-sell process.	2 hours
4) If this book has been helpful, give them a copy.	30 minutes
5) Engage your practice attorney to help facilitate the transfer of ownership. Start that conversation early as well.	2 hours
Succession Planning Total	**7 hours**

Section IV: People

Chapter 10 – Human Resources	Time Estimate
1) Calculate your group's turnover for the past year. If 10% or less, congratulate yourself! If >10%, get to work on this list right away.	30 minutes
2) Consider your group's prevailing attitude towards staff. Need some course corrections there? If so, discuss with your partners.	30 minutes
3) Take a look at your compensation across the board. It's good to graph this so you can see where everyone is relative to one another. Has everyone's compensation level been reviewed within the last year? Is it fair, given years of experience and level of contribution to the clinic? If not, make adjustments – pay raises only, not cuts, which are horribly demoralizing.	60 minutes
4) If it's been more than three months since your last celebration, schedule one.	30 minutes
5) Discuss culture and performance with your partners and choose some actions to measure and drive toward high performance.	60 minutes
Human Resources Total	**3.5 hours**

Chapter 11 – Extenders	Time Estimate
1) Ask your front desk when the next available new patient appointment is. If more than 3 weeks across the board, begin the work to add another partner or a mid-level.	60 minutes
2) Determine if another physician is warranted, or if a mid-level is the right addition.	30 minutes
3) Complete the **ROI** carefully, with good data so you know what to expect.	60 minutes
4) Update and rework your **Employment Agreement** as necessary for this new hire.	60 minutes
5) Get to recruiting. Expect this to take many months, so start early!	10-12 hours
Extenders Total	**13.5 – 15.5 hours**

Chapter 12 – Partnership	Time Estimate
1) If you're being invited into a partnership, do your due diligence! Request reports and schedule meetings and make sure that you understand who you are partnering with, and how the business has been run. Partnership can seem sexy and seductive from the outside…	5 hours
2) If you're offering partnership to a young associate, have the authentic conversations about Owner DNA, and what it takes to succeed. Many have a glossy version of partnership in their head (see #1 above), and lack a realistic understanding of the hard work involved. Beware the Gen X tendency to write off all millennials as unfit for ownership – many are fit, and just need some coaching.	3 hours
3) When figuring out your profit share, ensure that it is fair to all concerned and that you are in compliance with state and federal regulations. If you're now a senior partner in a comp formula that has unfairly favored senior partners to the detriment of junior ones, consider evolving that more towards the center. Again, a small investment with your practice attorney will alleviate a great deal of business risk here.	3 hours
Partnership Total	**5 – 6 hours**

Section V: Wrapping it All Up

Chapter 13 – Miscellany	Time Estimate
1) Make sure your practice employs several different payment mechanisms. If you don't have at least three, add some.	60 minutes
2) Check in on your payment plan and collections policies and be sure they are consistently applied and that they match your personal philosophy. Value your time here.	60 minutes
3) Check to see if your group uses Cash or Accrual accounting.	30 minutes
4) If you've seen or heard of some Phantom Profits within your group, be sure that you understand it.	30 minutes
5) Use paid professionals well – not too much and not too little, and don't fall into the trap of feeling like you need to figure everything out on your own. If your list of thought partners seems short, make an effort to reach out to a new colleague or mentor whom you admire and open a conversation.	2 hours
Miscellany Total	**5 hours**

GLOSSARY OF TERMS

Term	Definition	Page(s)
Accounts Receivable (A/R)	This represents all of the money that others owe to you for services you've provided for your patients.	41, 52, 53, 56, 60, 61
Advanced Payment Mechanisms	Online payment tools such as your website, a patient portal for payments, credit card vaulting, e-statements, and many others. Take two and call me in the morning.	109
Aged Accounts Receivable	This shows your total Accounts Receivable (the money people owe you for services already rendered) divided into Insurance balances and Patient balances. The first is for claims that have gone out to insurance companies, but have not yet been collected. The latter is for bills that have gone out to patients on patient statements, but have not yet been collected. The report will also be split up at a high level by types of payers, so you should have categories for Commercial Insurance, Medicare, Medicaid, Motor Vehicle Accidents (MVA), and Workers Compensation (WC). This will be further divided into aging "buckets" usually labeled as follows: 0-30 days (or Current), 31-60 days, 61-90 days, 91-120 days, 121-150 days, 151-180 days and 180+ days.	44, 56, 61
A/R Aging Report	See Aged Accounts Receivable.	57, 58, 59
Automated Clearing House (ACH)	Automated transactions that you initiate at your bank to send money electronically to another person or company.	49

Bad Debt	This is what is written off because patients fail to pay their bills. Also called Non-Contractual Adjustments.	54
Balance Sheet	A listing of your assets (what you have – think cash in your business checking account, equipment in your clinic), and your liabilities (what you owe – think credit card balances, loans). It is a snapshot in time, so it shows the balance in all accounts as of any given day.	4, 6, 10, 11, 113
Bank account reconciliation	Each bank account each month should be reconciled so that the amounts in QuickBooks match the amounts on the bank statement. Typically performed by the manager or bookkeeper, and should be reviewed and signed off on by one of the owners.	47
Beginning A/R Balance	This is the amount in your Accounts Receivable at the beginning of the month or time period.	53
Bottom Line	See Net Income.	7, 11
Bottom-Line Income	See Net Income.	7
Break Even Analysis	Analysis that tells you how much time it will take to recoup your initial investment – usually measured in months.	35, 37
Budget to Actual	A comparison of how your clinic performed financially with actual performance compared to the budget you originally created. This usually includes an analysis of any material variance from budget.	30, 31, 33
Business Owners Policy (BOP)	An insurance product that protects you from employee theft, wrongful termination (to a minimal degree – see Employment Practices Liability Insurance), and other general business risks to the business owner.	76

Calendar year deductible	Amount a patient must pay out of pocket before the insurance coverage kicks in. These vary widely based on plan, market, and plan design. Typical amounts are $1,000 – $3,000 per year.	29
Capital Asset Purchases	A purchase that the owner expects to hold for more than a year, and is not bought or sold in the normal course of business.	74
Certified Professional Coder (CPC)	Designation for someone who has completed a formal training course on coding and documentation standards, and has completed a successful apprenticeship.	14
Clean claim	A claim that goes all the way through and gets paid by the insurance company the first time. (Yay!)	53
Contractual Adjustments	This is how much was written off when the insurance companies paid you, and represents the delta between your billed Conversion Factor (usually $90 or higher) and your contracted rate with the insurance company (usually $55 – $75).	54, 56
Conversion Factor	Amount a practice charges per RVU, and also the amount an insurance company will pay per RVU.	7, 20, 22, 56
Cost of capital	When borrowing money for a purchase or expenditure, this is how much interest you will have to pay.	34, 74
Cost of Goods Sold	This is the invoice price you paid for any item that you resell in your clinic.	42
Cost of Living Adjustment (COLA)	An adjustment that reflects the increases in the cost of goods and services (a gallon of milk, a gallon of gas, average rent prices, etc.) in a given metro area for each year.	89
Cyber Liability	An insurance product that provides protection for medical practices against cyber attacks, ransomware, and data	77

	breaches.	
Daily cash balancing	Each person who receives payments from patients at the clinic should have a cash drawer or box that they balance each day. The total they took in (cash, checks, and credit cards) should be "batched" and should match what they entered into the practice management system.	47
Days in Accounts Receivable	Industry metric that seeks to answer (in days) how long it takes for you to collect the money you earned from the patients you saw today. In highly performing practices, we'd expect to see that number in the 20-30-day range.	59, 60, 61
Electronic Funds Transfer (EFT)	Payments being sent directly to your bank account from the insurance companies.	47, 48
Employment Agreement	A contract for employment that is written between the clinic and any provider or executive level employee.	98, 100
Employment Practices Liability Insurance (EPLI)	An insurance product that protects you past what your Business Owners Policy (BOP) does from wrongful termination or harassment lawsuits and provides for defense costs and settlements too.	76, 77
Ending A/R Balance	This is the amount in your Accounts Receivable at the end of the month or time period. Should always match the Beginning A/R Balance for the following period.	54
Evergreen contract	A term for a contract that continually renews until one of the parties formally terminates it.	19
Fixed Expenses	Expenses that are the same each month.	23
General Liability	See Property & Casualty (P&C).	76

Global periods	Defined by insurance companies as a time period in which all services are covered with one payment. Most common with surgeries and OB care.	59
Gross Charges	What was billed to the insurance companies and patients.	7, 44, 53, 56, 60
Gross Income	See Gross Revenue.	7
Gross Revenue	This is how much cash landed in your bank account. Also called Gross Income or Top Line Revenue.	7, 29, 113
Income Statement	A detail of all the income that came in during the time period, and all the expenses you incurred in the same time period. The amount left over is called "net income," and in most private practices is the amount that gets split up between the owners. Also called a Profit and Loss Statement (P&L).	6, 9
Internal controls	These are processes that are put into place in a business to protect owners from embezzlement, and to protect employees from being suspected of embezzlement.	45, 47, 49, 50, 51
Limited Liability Company (LLC)	A common legal construct that attempts to shield the owner of the company from personal liability for the company's debts or actions.	75
Lockbox	A special PO Box that is set up to receive your checks, which are then deposited directly into your bank account by a licensed, bonded, and insured person.	47, 48
Mission	Who you are… why you exist as an organization… your raison d'etre.	66, 67, 68
Net Income	This is Net Revenue less all expenses paid to run the clinic, before the doctors are paid. Also called Bottom Line or Bottom-Line Income.	6, 7, 113

Net Revenue	This is Gross Revenue less any money leaving your bank account in the form of refunds issued to insurance companies and patients.	7
Non-Contractual Adjustments	See Bad Debt.	54
Non-disclosure agreement (NDA)	A legal form that is used when two groups are entering into serious negotiations for purchase or sale, or when other highly confidential data will be shared or exchanged.	81
Occurrence-based policy	A type of medical malpractice generally held by large groups and health systems that does not require tail coverage.	77
Operational Plan	Action items for the next year from your strategic planning session listed in priority order with due dates and accountabilities.	69, 70, 72
Overhead Percentage	This is calculated as: Total Expenses divided by Net Revenue, and generally, anything lower than 50% is excellent.	7
Payments	This is how much money was posted into your Practice Management system during the month, and should match your bank deposits for the same time period.	47, 48, 49, 53, 54, 56
Practice Management (PM) software	Software that is used to register your patients, record their demographic information, schedule their appointments, create insurance claims, and track your Accounts Receivable.	42, 47, 49, 52, 53, 57, 59
Profit and Loss Statement (P&L)	See Income Statement.	4, 6, 10, 11, 22, 29, 30, 38, 113, 114

Property & Casualty (P&C)	An insurance product that protects the practice and you from a lawsuit filed by someone who was injured while at the clinic. This is commonly referred to as "slip and fall" coverage and it is routine for every business. Also called General Liability.	20, 76
QuickBooks	Gold standard accounting program – offered either online or in a local version, also called a desktop version. Manufactured by Intuit. Competitors are Zero, Sage, Freshbooks and others.	3, 10, 23, 30, 38, 42, 47
Refunds	Any amounts returned to the insurance companies or the patients out of your bank account due to an overpayment.	7, 29
Relative Value Unit (RVU)	Unit of measure used by the Centers for Medicare & Medicaid Services (CMS) to value each type of visit. Published annually by CPT code in the Federal Register in November or December. Tables can be downloaded from cms.gov.	7, 12, 19, 20, 22
Resource Based Relative Value System (RBRVS) Year	Listing from CMS of the CPT codes that are valid for each year, and the Relative Value Unit (RVU) ascribed to each one. This table also shows the components of the RVU and the expected payment from CMS for Medicare beneficiaries. It can be downloaded from cms.gov.	19, 22, 25
Return on Investment (ROI)	Calculation that shows what percentage of your initial investment will be returned to you in terms of increased revenue in the first year.	14, 35, 36, 74, 97, 98, 100, 118
Revenue cycle manager	Title for the person who manages your billing department.	14
Tail coverage	Part of your medical malpractice which may be assessed when you leave the practice to cover residual issues that	77

	may become lawsuits.	
Timely Filing Deadline	Length of time you have from the date of service to submit a claim to the insurance company. If you file your claim after this date, they WILL NOT PAY YOU, even though you did the work.	19
Top Line Revenue	See Gross Revenue.	7
Total Expenses	This is all of the money that left the bank account to pay for staff, rent, medical supplies, and any other expense to run the clinic. This DOES NOT include compensation for the physicians, even if you have some (or all) on salary.	7
Unrestricted personal guarantees	A document from your bank that requires you to guarantee the debt of the business, even if the business fails. Be aware of what you are signing!	103
Values	What you hold important on the journey to your vision... how you will behave.	66, 67, 68
Variable Expenses	Expenses that move up and down based on how busy the clinic is or how much volume goes through in a month.	23
Vision	Who you will be... what you strive for... your end goal.	66, 67, 68

ABOUT THE AUTHOR

Jill Arena wants your practice to be financially healthy.

She began her career as an auditor in a Big 8 public accounting firm way back in the day, where she learned all about managing the finances of businesses large and small. She transitioned into healthcare thirty years ago and has been running medical groups of various shapes and sizes ever since. She has held positions ranging from Clinic Manager to CEO.

Jill routinely presents to, and serves as advisor on, physician boards and executive committees. She enjoys walking with physician owners on their journey to run their businesses and develop their legacies. She has built a national consulting and revenue cycle company, which has served hundreds of medical groups across the country, and she speaks frequently at healthcare conferences. She loves to travel, entertain friends and family with gourmet meals, and hang out with her daughter, Bella and their crazy Labradoodle, Shaggy.